Six-month anniversary? I didn't know there was any such thing."

Cooper punched Ryan in the arm. "Excuse me? Of course there is such a thing and it's next Wednesday just so you know. I thought maybe we could do something romantic?" she suggested hopefully. "I know it's not a big deal to you, but it's important to me. If you do this I'll leave you alone about going to the museum with me next weekend."

That did it. Cooper had said the magic words.

"Just tell me when to pick you up, and leave the rest of the plans to me, my dear. One six-month anniversary dinner coming up."

Cooper smiled happily. This was going to be good...

NUMBER 4

SPRING BREAK

BY WENDY LEE NENTWIG

SPRING BREAK
published by Palisades
a part of the Questar publishing family

© 1996 by Wendy Lee Nentwig
International Standard Book Number: 0-88070-950-2

Cover photography by Mike Houska
Cover designed by Kevin Keller

Printed in the United States of America.

For information:
QUESTAR PUBLISHERS, INC.
POST OFFICE BOX 1720
SISTERS, OREGON 97759

96 97 98 99 00 01 02 03 — 10 9 8 7 6 5 4 3 2 1

ACKNOWLEDGEMENTS

I would be in big trouble if I did not thank the people who have kept me sane while I spent too many hours chained to my computer. So thanks to my family for still being excited for me and looking the other way when I wore the same pair of overalls for several days in a row or asked "have you read it yet?" for the millionth time. Thanks to my friends who read this manuscript when it was still a typo-riddled mess and pretended to like it anyway or kindly said nothing at all (that would be Jana Bedley Miller and Lisa Hausdorfer respectively). And thanks to my other friends, especially the real Penny and Brian, who encouraged, e-mailed, and asked impatiently when it would be in bookstores. Thanks to Robin Jones Gunn for passing my name along when Questar was looking for writers and to Lisa Tawn Bergren for giving me a chance. I won't forget it. But most of all to Shari MacDonald, editor extraordinaire and bestselling author in her own right: THANKS! (I know it seems like such a tiny word, but imagine it in 72 point type.) CBA would have been no fun at all without you (and Duane!). And finally, to the Great Author and Finisher who continues to love a very flawed me for reasons I can't begin to comprehend. Thank you, thank you, thank you for sending your son!

1

Cooper Ellis's alarm pierced the quiet just as the sunshine began peeking through the blinds of her dorm room window. Cooper let out a loud groan and slapped unsuccessfully at the snooze button.

As the offending alarm continued to blare, she sat up, reached over, and turned it off with a sigh. It was just as well. She really didn't have time to snuggle back under the covers, even for just ten minutes. Ryan would be pounding on her door soon enough and for reasons she had trouble remembering so early in the morning, she had promised she'd be ready.

An all-day hike on Mt. Rainier hadn't seemed like such a bad idea the other night when Ryan suggested it. They had been sitting in a quiet corner of The Cup & Chaucer, the coffeehouse where they had their first sort-of-date last September, and Ryan had been trying to find a way to get Cooper outdoors, as usual.

She had hoped the conversation might take a more romantic turn, but after almost six months together Cooper was beginning to understand that for Ryan, talking about the great wide open *was* romantic.

"Let's go rock climbing this weekend," he suggested.

"Not gonna happen," Cooper quickly replied. She tried to be open to new experiences, but she also knew her limitations and a lack of athletic ability was definitely one of them. In her opinion, someone who almost flunked gym class, not once but twice, had no business hanging from the side of a mountain. She tried to ignore Ryan's pleading look as she held her ground.

"I can't believe you came all the way across the country to go to college in the most beautiful place on earth and you never go outside! Why did you even bother to leave New York City if you aren't going to enjoy the Pacific Northwest?" he questioned, sounding exasperated.

"I go outside!" Cooper protested. "I walk to the cafeteria, to the library, and to all my classes. I must walk from one end of the campus to the other at least five times a day," she pointed out smugly. "And what about last week when we spent the entire afternoon studying at the park?"

When he still looked skeptical, she added, "Besides, I never said I came here for the scenery. Maybe I left New York just so I could meet you." As she said it, she looked up at him through big brown eyes and innocently batted her thick lashes.

He smiled and seemed to melt a little, but still he didn't give up.

"How about a nice tame hike then? The roads leading to Mt. Rainier's higher trails are still closed for the winter, but we can drive up to Palisades Inn and hike *around* the mountain. There are waterfalls and glaciers, and I bet you've never stood on a real volcano before."

"You say that like it's a bad thing," Cooper joked, but she could feel herself starting to cave.

"C'mon, it'll be great up there this time of year," Ryan urged.

"I guess a short hike wouldn't be that bad," Cooper found

herself saying. Before she had even finished her cappuccino, she had given in, like she had so many times since meeting Ryan during her first week at Pacific Cascades University. He was a year older and had been her orientation group leader, so it just seemed natural to let him be in charge of things. Besides, Ryan had grown up just a few hours south of Seattle, so he knew the area, and she was happy to let him show her around.

Cooper stood motionless in the shower, trying not to think about how early it was as she let the hot water run over her in streams. Cooper had never been good with mornings. She had even worked out her schedule so none of her classes started before ten. It had taken a little rearranging, but it was worth it. Ryan, on the other hand, had an eight o'clock class every single morning and even managed to stop by the cafeteria on his way. Cooper hadn't made it to breakfast once the entire first semester.

Quietly, she finished getting ready. At the sound of Ryan's knock, the form in the other bed rolled over. Cooper was trying to make her way silently across the room when she heard her roommate Emily's muffled voice from under her thick, green quilt.

"Don't have too much fun with that brother of mine."

Cooper grunted in response, although if it had been a more civilized hour she would have smiled at Emily's friendly teasing.

Their relationship hadn't always been so comfortable. When Cooper and Ryan started dating, Emily was less than thrilled. After years of living under her overachieving brother's shadow, she had hoped to put a little space between them at college. A romance between Ryan and her new roommate was not part of the plan. Emily still wasn't always comfortable with the situation. But while working through it, the girls had gone from being roommates to friends.

"All ready?" Ryan asked, much too cheerfully, before the door was fully open. In response, Cooper leaned sleepily against the doorframe. Ryan ignored her lack of enthusiasm.

"Where's your stuff?" he asked, apparently anxious to get on the road.

"I've got everything in my backpack," she answered, holding up the small Levi's pack she used to carry books from one end of campus to the other.

"That is not a backpack, it's a large purse," Ryan pointed out bluntly.

"Well, if you don't think I have the right equipment, I guess we'll just have to stay home," Cooper countered, noticeably perking up at the thought.

"Oh, no you don't! This will work for today, but we'll have to see about getting you a real day pack for next time," Ryan told her, holding on to her arm as if he were afraid she might try to escape. "Now do you have enough layers on?"

"Tank top, long-sleeved T-shirt, denim shirt, pullover," she listed off, pulling the bottom hem of each item out from under her jacket to show him as she went along. "I borrowed the jacket from your sister last night," she explained, zipping up the lined, red anorak. Actually, most of what she was wearing was Emily's. Cooper felt like she should have been posing for an Eddie Bauer ad. At least the shoes were her own.

At that moment Ryan looked down and, taking in her black canvas tennis shoes, asked, "Don't you have any hiking boots?"

"If I did, do you think your sister would have let me get away with wearing these?" Cooper asked, trying to keep the sarcasm out of her voice. "Emily's feet are a size smaller than mine, so it's either these or sandals. I have a really nice pair of cross-trainers I got last summer, but I left them in New York. They were just too white and normal looking. I always felt weird in them."

Ryan let the subject drop, ushering Cooper into the hall and out toward the parking lot. Once inside the old, gray truck, she curled up next to him and leaned her head against his shoulder, planning to nap during the two-and-a-half-hour drive.

"You're not going to sleep, are you?" Ryan asked, incredulous. "This is the best time of day, with the sun coming up behind the mountains. If you fall asleep you'll miss it."

"I'm going to ignore that 'best time of day' comment because it's too early for me to argue with you intelligently. But, yes, I am planning to sleep. And if you want me to be any fun when we get there, you should let me close my eyes."

"You weren't kidding about not being a morning person, were you?"

Cooper sighed. "No, I would never kid about something as important to me as sleep. And I want you to know you are one of the only people I would get up for at this hour. You should feel honored," she told him, then added, "but would you mind feeling honored while I get some sleep?"

In answer, Ryan kissed the top of Cooper's head, and she settled in against him for the long ride. But just before drifting off, she couldn't resist trying one last time to get out of their excursion.

"You know, it's still not too late to go grab some bagels and spend a fun-filled day at the museum."

Cooper's eyes were closed, but she could hear Ryan making loud gagging noises. She snuggled closer and dozed off, a smile playing on her lips.

She was in a decidedly better mood when Ryan woke her. As she looked out the truck's front windshield she had to duck her head almost to dashboard level in order to see the snow-covered tip of Mt. Rainier.

"So, what do you think?" Ryan asked.

"It's beautiful!" Cooper exclaimed excitedly.

"Didn't I tell you?" Ryan responded with pride, as if he had created the awesome mountain himself.

Soon enough they were out of the truck and moving toward the trail. At first, time passed quickly, with Ryan pointing out different rock formations and other interesting bits of land-scape.

"It's amazing! You can see everything from here," Cooper said, staring off into the distance.

"Yeah. Seattle looks so far away, doesn't it?" Ryan said, pointing out the city's skyline.

The view alone was enough to keep her interested for a while, but eventually Cooper's feet were tired and she was ready for a break.

"Let's sit down for a while and have something to eat," she suggested, already stooping to lean against the rocky face of the mountain. Ryan, intent on the trail ahead, didn't hear her and kept moving quickly along the path.

When she was a good twenty-five feet behind Ryan and he still hadn't stopped, Cooper yelled after him. At the sound of her voice, Ryan finally turned.

"What are you doing way back there?" he called to her.

"I'm ready for a break," Cooper explained, trying not to sound annoyed. "We've been walking for almost two hours and I need a snack. Also, I want to rest my feet for a few minutes."

"Are you serious?" Ryan asked.

"Don't I look serious?" she countered. Cooper was in good shape and could have continued on, but she hadn't eaten breakfast and she saw no reason to race up the mountain. They had all day, although she hoped they wouldn't be hiking quite that long.

Slowly Ryan made his way back to where Cooper was, but

it was evident he wasn't happy to be taking a break so soon.

Cooper pulled a rice cake out of her pack and crunched into it, then offered a bite to her boyfriend. Ryan wrinkled up his nose.

"You're not going to get much energy from that Styrofoam," he told her. "Didn't you bring anything else? Some fruit or granola bars? I have some beef jerky in my pack if you want a piece."

"I'm fine," Cooper answered, pushing her sunglasses up on her head like a headband so she could look at him. She really liked the taste of rice cakes, especially the caramel ones, but she could never convince Ryan of this. "I have an apple I'm saving for dessert," she offered, feeling the need to make up for the rice cakes in some way.

They climbed up on a large rock with a view of a trickling mini-waterfall. As she ate, Cooper watched the melting snow running down the side of the mountain in a crevice carved out by years and years of the same. She wished they could stay there forever. It was so peaceful and beautiful. Certainly nothing like New York City, even in Central Park. All too soon, though, Ryan was on his feet, looking impatient to get going.

The day continued on like that, with Ryan racing ahead and Cooper lagging behind. Cooper wouldn't have minded so much if Ryan had been willing to follow her around once in a while, exploring the shops in Seattle's funky Fremont district, seeing a play, or even, as she had jokingly suggested, going to a museum. But he wasn't. It wasn't that he flatly refused to do the things she liked; it just seemed as if they never did those things together. Instead, Cooper would go shopping with Emily or their suitemate, Kenzie, or wander through the museums by herself.

"Are you sore at all?" Ryan asked, bringing Cooper back to

the present. She let her discontent fade away temporarily as they drove home, focusing on a discussion about her tired muscles and the trails Ryan wanted to cover on their next trip. He just assumed there would be a next trip. Cooper wished she felt that sure of things. Maybe next week she would try to bring up the museum again. Then again maybe not. She knew if he did go with her it would be because she made him and she probably wouldn't have any fun anyway.

Maybe I should just try to focus more on the things we do together that we really both enjoy, Cooper thought. But as she started making a mental list, she realized there weren't too many things on it.

2

It was dinnertime when Ryan dropped her off in front of her dorm with a quick goodnight kiss. "The guys" were going out that night to the batting cages so he had to hurry back to Mercer Hall and shower. Although Cooper felt grimy and her legs ached, she decided to run to the cafeteria and grab a quick salad and some yogurt. She planned to spend a boring night studying, and past experience told her that if she didn't eat dinner she would be raiding the vending machines in an hour or two, filling up on Chee-tos and Starbursts.

As she made her way stiffly to the cafeteria she heard someone calling her name. Cooper turned and, before she could pretend she didn't see him, realized it was the person she least wanted to bump into: Sam.

Sam was a perfectly nice guy, but he had a way of getting on Cooper's nerves. Just because they were both from New York City, the only two New Yorkers on the PCU campus in fact, he thought they should be friends. He was always talking about the Yankees or Washington Square Park or this great record store in SoHo that he used to go to all the time. All his reminiscing only served to remind her that she was probably the only person who didn't fit in in New York.

It was because of this that Cooper had *wanted* to get away and had spent years planning her escape. She had been anxious to come to Seattle and meet people who didn't want to be fashion designers or actors or film directors like everyone in her high school had wanted to be. She wanted a life more like that of her Aunt Penny, her mom's sister who lived just outside of Seattle and worked with teenage girls at a group home. Penny was doing something important, making a real difference in people's lives, and that was what Cooper wanted, too. Penny also had a great fiancé named Brian, who was a computer programmer and also taught a couple of classes at PCU. Cooper ran into him on campus a lot and she couldn't wait until his and Penny's wedding that summer, when he would really become Cooper's uncle at last.

"Are you grabbing some dinner, too?" Sam asked, falling into step with her. Cooper hadn't invited him, but it looked like they would be eating together.

She studied Sam as they stood in line to get one of the orange plastic trays that the cafeteria seemed to have in endless supply. His hair was the same dark shade as hers, and had the same bit of natural wave to it, but the similarities stopped there. While Cooper wore hers sleek and shoulder length, and fought each morning to make it as straight as possible, Sam let his hang naturally. It was almost as long as hers in back, but as he leaned forward his too-long bangs brushed his cheekbones. Cooper waited for him to push the hair back out of his eyes, but he didn't seem to even notice it was there.

"Are you getting in the hot-food line?" he asked suddenly, catching her off guard.

"Uh, no," she stammered. "I'm just having a salad."

"Me, too!" Sam answered triumphantly, as if their similar

taste in food gave them just one more reason to be friends. Cooper rolled her eyes as she led the way to the salad bar.

After they'd filled their trays, she began to scan the room for a familiar face. If she could find someone for them to sit with, Cooper figured, she wouldn't have to spend the whole meal alone with Sam. Unfortunately, the cafeteria was fairly deserted since it was Saturday night, so Cooper's plan never quite materialized. It wasn't that she didn't want to be seen with Sam—Cooper would sit with just about anybody in the cafeteria and had met some pretty cool people over lunch or dinner—she just knew how the meal would turn out.

It happened while they were discussing some assignments for the Beginning Photography class they were both taking. As he talked, Cooper was noticing how Sam had really clear gold eyes that seemed to look right into the core of her—or whoever he was talking to, she guessed—as if nothing could tear him away. He was talking about the film he'd shot the previous weekend at Pike's Place Market downtown, and as he described the color and textural contrast between the mounds of fish next to the buckets of fresh-cut flowers she couldn't help thinking that Sam could be sort of interesting when he wanted to be.

"So what do you think you'll pick for the subject of your photo essay?" she asked him. It was their final project for the class and wasn't due for a couple of months, but its grade would carry the most weight.

"New York City, no contest. I just can't imagine feeling as passionate about pictures of anywhere else. There's so much to photograph and even though it's all been done a million times it still looks new, you know?" Sam answered quickly, as if Cooper would be stupid not to choose that herself.

"Instead of taking pictures of all the usual landmarks, though, I'm going to take pictures from their point of view.

What the Statue of Liberty sees, the top of the Empire State Building looking out on the city, stuff like that. When I go home for spring break next month, I figure I'll shoot around two rolls a day. That should give me more than enough to pick from."

Cooper sensed that she was beginning to tune Sam out. It wasn't that she hated New York, but sometimes she felt as though New York hated her. Everyone was so busy there, and they all seemed to conspire against Cooper to emphasize her own lack of purpose in life. Sure, her parents and her friends were encouraging, telling her she didn't have to know how she wanted to spend the rest of her life when she was still only eighteen. But that was easy for them to say. They all knew what they wanted to do. And until she had a little more direction, Cooper felt that she would rather not be in New York for any extended period of time.

"So are you going home for spring break?" Sam asked, as if on cue. Apparently he was done with his "ode to New York City," at least temporarily.

"No, I'm going to my boyfriend's in Central Oregon for the week," Cooper said with a smile. She was really looking forward to seeing what life was like away from any big cities, imagining people out on front porches sipping lemonade and big lawns where kids ran through the sprinklers and pitched tents in the summer. All the things she never had growing up.

"Really?" Sam said, looking a little surprised.

"What? Why are you looking at me like that?" Cooper asked, annoyed by what she interpreted as a slight look of disapproval.

"Nothing!" Sam protested, holding up his hands in surrender. He seemed genuinely taken aback. "It just seems so soon to meet the family, don't you think? I didn't know things were that serious," he explained. Then he added a little more quietly, "So you really like this guy, huh?"

"For your information it's not like I'm going to meet his parents to announce our engagement or anything. Also, we've been dating for six months so it's not 'so soon.' 'So soon' would have been if I had gone home with him for Thanksgiving, which I didn't. I'm just not all that excited about going back to New York for Easter, so I took Ryan up on his invitation, not that it's any of your business."

"You're right, it isn't any of my business. But since you're answering anyway, you didn't get to my last question. Do you really like this guy that much?"

Cooper took a deep breath and exhaled slowly, trying to calm down before answering Sam's question.

"Of course I really like him! Why would I go out with someone for six months if I didn't really like him?" Cooper asked. But even as she answered so emphatically, doubts began to creep in: doubts about their little arguments all day at Mt. Rainier, the disagreements over what to do every weekend, the feeling she had more frequently of always being the one to give in. *But Ryan's a great guy!* she thought to herself. "He's a great guy!"

When Sam looked at her quizzically she realized she had said that last part out loud. *Oops!*

"Well he is," she added defensively. Sam didn't answer; he just raised one dark eyebrow before taking another bite of pasta salad. The conversation was almost nonexistent after that, and as Cooper walked back to her dorm later she was still fuming.

What right did he have to ask me all kinds of personal questions and force me to defend my relationship with Ryan? None. No right at all. So why did she suddenly feel so uncertain?

Back in her dorm room, Cooper tried to focus on her

Human Behavior textbook, but it was no use. She didn't find the class all that interesting when she *wasn't* distracted. Eager for a diversion, she grabbed her laptop off her desk and began the process of checking her e-mail. The hardest thing about moving away from New York had been leaving her two best friends, Claire and Alex. But both of them sent her messages by computer almost daily, so she always knew what was going on in their lives and vice-versa.

Cooper hooked up her modem and heard the comforting hum of it dialing the local access number. In less than a minute she was looking at a letter from Claire.

Claire was the perfect New Yorker. She was in her first year studying fashion design at Parson's in Greenwich Village, but she had been making her own clothes for years. She had always known what she wanted to do and had already sold some of her designs at the trendy little clothing store where she worked a few hours a week. Her message was full of news about school and what projects she was working on and which teachers she loved and with which designers she hoped to get an internship that summer. Also, she was excited about Fashion Week, the semi-annual fashion shows that soon would be taking over New York City's Bryant Park.

"You know how you have to have an invitation to get in, especially to the bigger shows, right?" Claire asked in her letter. "Well the older design students have all sorts of ways to get around that, so it looks like I'll actually get a peek at what's on the runways this year instead of having to wait and read about it in *Women's Wear Daily* or *Vogue.* Can you believe it?"

Of course Cooper could believe it, and she was happy for Claire, but her friend's letter only intensified Cooper's feelings about her lack of direction. Cooper leaned back against her pillow and wished for the millionth time that she could be as sure as Claire was about what came next in life.

Cooper wrote back, telling Claire about her hiking trip, but leaving out the parts about getting up before dawn and the little disagreements she'd had with Ryan. Her friends already thought she was crazy for leaving New York in the first place. She didn't want to give them any reason to think she was unhappy with her choice. There wasn't a message from Alex, but Claire mentioned him several times in her note.

"I took Alex to a movie at the Angelika last night to celebrate the 'A' he got on an assignment for his scriptwriting class," she explained, referring to the artsy theater near New York University that was their friend's favorite. "To pay me back, he's bringing some videos over tonight. I think the theme is 'Former TV Stars Who Became Successful Directors' or something like that. You know Alex."

Cooper sure did. Alex's obsession with movies had begun long before he'd decided to study film at NYU. As a result, he could never just *enjoy* a movie. Every one was an event. Alex would read Cooper and Claire reviews during lunch period or copy articles out of *Premiere Magazine* or the *New York Times* for them to look over in study hall. He would even quiz them on the way to the theater to make sure they had done the required reading. It would have been annoying coming from anyone else, but they forgave it in Alex. And they both had to admit that whenever they saw movies without him, it just wasn't the same.

Just as Cooper plugged her phone back into the jack she had been using for her modem it rang loudly, startling her so much she almost dropped the receiver. When she did finally manage to lift it to her ear, she was happy to hear her aunt's voice on the other end.

"Your line's been busy for the last half-hour. Talking to

someone fun, I hope?" Aunt Penny queried.

"Oh, sorry. I had my modem plugged in. I was just keeping in touch with the gang back in New York."

"Well that's good to hear. I thought maybe you had cut all ties there."

"Of course not. Just because I don't want to live in New York right now doesn't mean I don't still have friends there. Besides, Mom would never let me get away with that. Do you know what she sent me the other day? A bottle of Chanel nail polish from Bloomingdale's with a note explaining that it was a new spring color and she didn't know if we would be getting it here. Penny, she acts like we live on the moon!"

"As far as she's concerned, we do," her aunt laughed. "And in some ways maybe she's right. "It's not New York, that's for sure."

"Which is fine with me," Cooper responded. "I have to say, though, it was a great nail polish color."

"That sister of mine always did have good taste."

"I still think one of you had to be adopted. I mean there is just no way you can really be related," Cooper said.

"Oh, we're more alike than you think, Cooper. Just remember I'm twelve years younger than your mother. You give me awhile, and I'll be sending you nail polish, too."

"I doubt that."

"We'll see," Aunt Penny said. "Anyway, I wasn't calling to discuss the family tree. I wanted to know if you're coming to church with us in the morning. I thought with the hike today you might be too tired."

"Oh, no. I'm a little sore, but nothing a hot bath won't fix. Anyway, we got back early because Ryan had plans tonight, so I'm definitely there," Cooper added.

"Great, then I'll get to work on a lasagna right now. Brian

was bugging me to make one, but I told him I'd only do it if you were coming over. It's too much work for just the two of us. But for you I'll—" Her last few words were drowned out.

"What did you say?" Cooper asked, straining to hear over an unidentifiable noise in the background.

"Sorry, Brian's over and he's yelling that if you come over there won't be any leftovers for him. Ignore him."

Cooper just laughed in response.

"Isn't he awful, Cooper?" Penny continued. "That man lives to eat. I don't know what I'm going to do when we get married. There will never be a morsel of food in the house. I'll have to grocery shop every day!"

Hunh, Cooper thought. *Maybe I don't want Aunt Penny's life after all.*

3

xcept for a few quick lunches in the cafeteria, Cooper didn't see Ryan again until Wednesday night at The Cup & Chaucer. He had basketball practice every day during the week so there wasn't much time after classes and homework to just hang out, and Cooper was busy studying for her upcoming midterms anyway. But they always had a standing date—sort of a group date—on Wednesday, when they would meet up with a bunch of their friends at the group's favorite coffeehouse, near the campus.

Upon arrival, Cooper headed to their usual table near the back, next to a shelf lined with old books.

Ryan was already there, and so were Emily and Dan. And Cooper wasn't sure, but it looked like Emily and Dan might be holding hands under the table. Upon closer examination, she realized that her roommate seemed to have taken a little extra time with her curly brown hair and was wearing more make-up than usual, too. Cooper would have to ask for details as soon as she and Emily were alone. Ethan, a freshman who had been in Ryan's orientation group with Cooper, was also at the table, but

Kenzie Dawson, Cooper and Emily's suitemate, was missing.

"Where's our sixth wheel?" Cooper asked as she took a seat on a squishy blue velvet couch next to Ryan.

"She and Chris are rehearsing for an open mike night they're going to play at somewhere this weekend," Ethan explained. He and Kenzie were both from Tennessee and had grown pretty close over the course of the school year, so Cooper could always count on him for an update on her suite-mate's life.

"Did they finalize the dates they're playing at The Cup yet?" Ryan queried.

"They play two sets next Saturday night," Ethan reported proudly, pushing his round wire-frame glasses up on his nose. "And if that goes well they'll be regulars." Like dozens of other PCU students, Ethan would—upon rare occasion—bring his guitar to The Cup to dabble at songwriting with his friends. He was not a performer, as were Kenzie and Chris. But he shared their excitement, as if it were his own.

"That's so great!" Emily chimed in. Everyone had been sur- prised to find out almost six months into the school year that Kenzie was amazingly talented on the guitar, since no one had ever even seen her pick up an instrument until then. As the daughter of a major Christian music mogul from Nashville, she had kept her identity—and talent—secret right up until Valentine's Day.

Some people thought it was weird that Kenzie didn't want people to know what her dad did, and that she didn't use his contacts to get a record deal for herself or Chris, a PCU student who was equally talented and who Cooper knew Kenzie had more than a little crush on. For reasons of her own, Cooper understood, though.

When the guys went to the counter to get refills, Cooper

leaned over to her roomie and said, "I thought you and Dan were just friends, Em? You look pretty cozy to me."

Emily turned bright red at her friend's observation. She and Dan had met the first week of school when Emily started dating his friend John. John had turned out to be a jerk, but Dan and Emily had become friends, so something good came out of the whole mess. At first, Dan had wanted them to be more than friends and had even sent Emily some flowers and notes anonymously. Finally, he had asked her out and admitted to being her secret admirer, but at the time Emily wasn't quite ready for another relationship. Also, Dan had just started coming to church, and Em wanted to give his new faith some time to grow.

"Well?" Cooper prompted, impatient for details before the subject of her inquiry returned to the table.

"Well, we had a really nice time on his birthday and I finally decided that I was ready to take the next step. I mean, I've thought of him as more than a friend for a long time now, I was just afraid to admit it."

"So you're a couple then!" Cooper announced.

"No, we're dating," Emily corrected. Cooper grinned and gave her roommate a hug. Then, noticing the guys crossing the room, she sat back in her chair and tried to wipe the smile off her face.

"So, that history test sure was hard," Cooper said in an exaggerated tone, pretending they had been talking about studying the whole time the guys were gone. They might have been believed it, too, if only Emily hadn't blurted out "What history test? You're not even taking history this semester!"

Cooper groaned in Emily's direction. "What am I going to do with you?"

Emily just smiled good-naturedly. She never was very good

at playing games. If she was interested in someone she couldn't pretend she wasn't, and it was obvious she was interested in Dan.

To look at Dan, with his dark hair pulled back in a ponytail and his beat-up Doc Marten's, Cooper never would have guessed that he and the conservative Emily would get along so well. But he was the nicest guy, and he was so excited about his new faith.

"Glad you finally figured it out," Cooper leaned over and whispered in Emily's ear.

"Excuse me, what was that you said?" Ryan teased, cupping a hand to his own ear so he could hear better. "Why not share it with the whole table? Don't you know it's rude to whisper?"

The girls ignored him and focused on their drinks, Emily gulping down a hot chocolate with tons of whipped cream while Cooper sipped the cafe mocha Ryan had brought her.

"You know," Cooper said, trying to change the subject once and for all, "that our six-month anniversary is coming up next week, Ryan Stewart."

"Six-month anniversary? I didn't know there was any such thing."

Cooper punched Ryan in the arm. "Excuse me? Of course there is such a thing and it's next Wednesday just so you know. I thought maybe we could do something romantic?" she suggested hopefully. "I know it's not a big deal to you, but it's important to me. If you do this I'll leave you alone about going to the museum with me next weekend."

That did it. Cooper had said the magic words.

"Just tell me when to pick you up, and leave the rest of the plans to me, my dear. One six-month anniversary dinner coming up."

Cooper smiled happily. This was going to be good...

That Sunday, on her way back to campus after church, Cooper stopped by a shop called The Perfect Bagel. She had found it during the first semester and had been coming back at least once a week ever since. Even Cooper had to admit that there was nothing like a New York bagel, and The Perfect Bagel shop had to be as close as a person could get outside of the Big Apple. As she waited for her order—a cinnamon raisin bagel with raisin walnut cream cheese—she glanced around the small shop. Just then their eyes met.

"Hey, Cooper! Homesick for a little taste of New York, huh?"

Cooper stifled a groan. It was Sam. She should have known it was only a matter of time before she ran into him here. After all it was a bagel shop, and what was more New York than that? He motioned her over to his table. Knowing that it would be rude not to go, she made her way across the room as if she were being led to the gallows. As she approached his table she offered a halfhearted "hey." It was the best she could do.

He motioned for her to sit down, but she declined.

"My order should be up in just a second," she explained.

"Oh," Sam replied, looking a little disappointed. "Did you just come from church?" he asked to Cooper's surprise.

"How did you know that?" she asked. Was he spying on her now?

"You have a church bulletin sticking out of your purse," he explained, pointing to the rose colored flyer with teal printing.

"Oh, right." Cooper said, embarrassed at her paranoia.

"Where do you go?" he asked.

"It's called Cornerstone. It's just outside of town, in Redmond. I like it, but I wish services were a little later," she confessed with a yawn. "My church in New York has its main service at three in the afternoon, and I like that so much better."

"I think that's the first time you've ever said anything good about New York since I've known you," Sam told her.

"I say good things about New York from time to time," Cooper told him. "I am just enjoying living somewhere else for a while…unlike you," she added pointedly. "Why did you leave New York if you love it so much?"

Sam stared down at a section of the newspaper spread out on the table, suddenly seeming to concentrate very hard on a headline. Cooper had a weird feeling she had said something wrong, but she didn't know why. She waited for Sam to explain, then was sorry when he did.

"It wasn't my idea, believe me. I was going to go to City University, but my little sister got sick again last year and my mom spent months practically living in her hospital room. I was fine, but my mom got this idea in her head that I needed to get away, that I was taking on too much responsibility and worrying too much. So here I am, three thousand miles away and hating every minute of it."

"Actually we're 2,419 miles from New York—I checked it out on my computer—but still, I'm really sorry," Cooper said and meant it. Now she felt horrible for being so unfriendly. She just had such a hard time being nice to Sam when he was always bringing up New York, the one thing that made her feel so inadequate, but at least now she understood a little better why he did it.

Sam just shrugged off her apology and looked down at his hands.

"Well, maybe you could transfer back next year," she suggested. "I mean, did your dad agree with her? My mom didn't want to let me come to PCU, but my dad helped me win her over."

"I don't think that will be happening," he said wryly. "My

dad left when my sister got sick the first time. The leukemia was too much for him to deal with, I guess, and we don't really see him much. He lives up in Connecticut."

"Oh," Cooper said, trying to imagine what Sam must have gone through. She knew she couldn't even begin to understand, though.

"You don't have to look so stricken. We're managing just fine, and Rachel should be out of the hospital the whole week I'm home...so that's cool."

"I guess," Cooper responded, trying to infuse her words with an optimism she didn't feel. Just then she heard her order number being called.

"Uh, I think that's you," Sam said, pointing toward the front counter.

"Yeah," Cooper agreed, but made no move to leave. It felt wrong to walk away, but she couldn't think of anything to say.

"Hey, if you're looking for a later service on Sunday you should give St. Mark's a try," Sam told her. "They're just up the street from campus, and they have something called a compline service late on Sunday night. I can't really explain it, but it's the most spiritual thing I've ever seen."

"A com-what service?"

"Compline. I think it literally means something to mark the end of the seven canonical hours or something. Basically, it's just a service to mark the end of the week, from what I can figure out," Sam explained.

"Sounds interesting. Maybe I'll do that," Cooper nodded before making her way to her waiting order at last.

"See you later, Sam," she called as she headed out the door. Once inside her car she found she wasn't very hungry after all. She left the bagel untouched in its bag and sped out of the parking lot toward the PCU campus.

4

ooper was still in a bit of a fog when she entered her dorm room, so it took her a few seconds to notice that Emily was not only talking, but talking to her.

"What?" Cooper asked distractedly.

An exaggerated sigh escaped from Emily's lips. "I said your mom called. I didn't really understand what she was talking about. It sounded like she said your bookie kept calling and you were supposed to call her back."

Cooper collapsed onto her bed and pulled a pillow over her head.

"I don't mean to pry, but isn't a bookie someone you place bets with?" Emily asked.

"Yes," Cooper answered, then paused for a long time before attempting to clear up the misunderstanding. "But don't worry, I don't have a bookie, I have a booker, which is something totally different."

"Oh, thanks for straightening that out for me," Emily replied sarcastically.

"It's a long story." Cooper paused. "Are you sure you want to hear it?"

"Of course," Emily said, joining her roommate on the bed. "You've got me all curious now."

"Well, a booker is like an agent for models. They book you for jobs, send your pictures around to everyone, all of that."

"I don't get it, then. Why do you have a booker?" Emily interrupted.

Cooper hugged her pillow to her stomach and took a deep breath before she launched into her story. "Well, you see, I have a booker, because I'm a model...or I used to be," she said, bracing herself for her roommate's reaction.

Emily looked at her in surprise. "You mean like in magazines?" she asked.

"Yeah, I've done a little editorial. I've also done some catalog work and a few ads. It's not like I've been in *Vogue* or anything," she explained.

"Still, I can't imagine ever making money off of how I look," Emily countered.

"Believe me, it's not as great as it sounds. If it was, I'd still be doing it."

"So why did you do it in the first place if you didn't want to?"

Cooper tried to collect her thoughts before answering. She had asked herself that same question many times and still wasn't completely sure.

"I was shopping with my mom one day and this woman approached us and asked if I ever modeled. We thought she was selling something, but she talked to us for a while and seemed to be on the level. She wasn't real pushy, she just gave us a business card and told me to call if I was interested and if it was okay with my parents. I felt a little weird about it, but my mom talked me into at least going to meet with them, and it turned into an after school job. I just never saw it as a career."

"You're not modeling anymore, are you? I mean, why do you have to call your booker? Haven't you already quit?" Emily asked.

"Not exactly. I just haven't been working since I started school. You see, I've always known modeling wasn't really for me long-term. I've always felt uncomfortable making money off my looks, but because I was able to break into the business so easily I've always thought there was some reason for it, some higher purpose. As sappy as it sounds, I truly believe God let me get into modeling for a reason, and it feels wrong to get out before I know what that reason is."

"That makes sense," Emily agreed.

"I can't quite imagine explaining all of this to my booker, Tara, though," Cooper said.

"So why don't you keep at it awhile longer?"

"I just don't think I can keep modeling without knowing I'm doing it for more than just the money. And now my agency wants me to go to Italy this summer to build up my book."

"Okay, you're talking a different language now. Back up and explain," Emily instructed. "What do you mean 'your book?'"

"A book is a collection of a model's work. It's filled with pages from magazines or catalogs that she's been in, as well as any other pictures she does. Agencies send them out to people who might want to hire models, so clients can see how they photograph and what different looks they're capable of. That way, the models don't waste so much time going to see about jobs they're definitely not right for. Although they do a lot of that, too."

"And you're turning down the chance to go to Italy?"

Cooper nodded emphatically. "Definitely. I don't want to spend a hot, sticky summer living in some crowded models' apartment and being told I'm not tall enough or old enough or that my eyes are the wrong shade of brown. It's depressing."

"But it's still Italy! Does Ryan know?"

"No," Cooper quickly answered, "and I'd like to keep it that way. When I first started working, I got teased by kids at school. And there were guys who just wanted to go out with me because they saw my picture somewhere. I know it wouldn't matter to Ryan, but I just don't think I want to be known for that."

Emily nodded. Cooper figured she probably understood. Their suitemate, Kenzie, had recently made a similar admission. As Kenzie had explained to Emily, she had hidden the truth about her father being the head of a major Christian music label because she wanted to be liked for who she was, not because of whom she knew. Cooper related to Kenzie's confession. She knew what it was like to wonder whether people were being nice to her because they really liked Cooper, or because of what she could do for them.

"That makes sense," Emily said. "So are you going to call this booker person back, though? Your mom seemed pretty adamant about it."

"That's because my mom likes having a daughter who's a model," Cooper replied a little coldly.

"I've never met your mother, but that sounds kind of harsh," Emily volunteered a bit meekly.

"Oh, I know," Cooper responded, "and I'm sure that deep down she just wants what's best for me. It's just that sometimes she pushes too hard. She has a hard time letting me figure things out for myself. She was really disappointed when I decided to go to college full time and give modeling up."

"Couldn't you still get back into modeling after you finish school if you decided you wanted to?" Emily asked.

Cooper shook her head. "Not really. It's kind of hard to

explain, but most agencies don't want to take anyone over twenty-one, so if my agency drops me—or if I drop them—it's not very likely I can go back in a few years and get someone to sign me," she explained. "That's why my mom didn't take it so well. She thinks I'm throwing away my future. She even took me on a trip last spring to visit an old friend of hers who lives in Paris and to go see some of the French agencies. She hoped that I would change my mind when I saw them, but I didn't. I loved Europe, but if I went there I don't think it would be to model."

"Why? I mean I know this is kind of rude, but couldn't you make a lot of money there?" Emily asked.

"Some girls do, of course, but there are so many more who are really struggling, living in these tiny apartments without refrigerators. In the winter they leave their food out on the fire escape to keep it cold and I don't know what they do in the summer. If I'm going to make those kind of sacrifices, it had better be for something more meaningful than getting my picture in a magazine."

"That's weird that your mom would think you're throwing your life away by going to college. Usually it's the other way around."

"That's exactly what I'm always trying to tell her!" Cooper cried, years of built-up tension creeping into her voice. Calming down a bit, she added, "I think I would be more convincing if I actually knew what I wanted to study, though. She's always trying to persuade me to keep modeling until I decide what I'd rather do. But I'm afraid if I do that I'll never figure out what I want to do with my life. At least now I can take classes and see what I like and what I don't."

"So are you finding anything you like?"

"Not really," Cooper had to admit. "But I have found out

this semester that I definitely *don't* like psychology, calculus, or chemistry so at least I'm narrowing it down a little."

"What classes does that leave?" Emily asked. "Any of them?"

"I like my photography class," Cooper offered. "As a matter of fact, I like that one a lot."

"Well you should definitely stick with that then. But can you major in photography?"

"I don't think so," Cooper told her. "It probably falls under the jurisdiction of the art department."

"Dan's an art major. You might want to talk to him about it," Emily suggested. "Remember those posters he made for me last semester, to promote my radio show? I bet I owe most of my listeners to him. He's really good, you know. His drawing teacher is letting him display some of his work in the end of the year show even though he's only a freshman."

"It's nice to know someone has his life figured out," Cooper said.

"I'm sorry. I wish I could be more helpful, but I still don't know what *I'm* going to major in."

"But at least you don't have my mother. If I know her, she'll be calling to check up on me tomorrow night, so it looks like I'll have to call my agency back." As Cooper said the words a feeling of dread crept over her. Would her life ever be her own?

5

Cooper put off making the phone call to the modeling agency for as long as she could. But when she returned to her dorm room after lunch on Monday, she knew she couldn't wait any longer. It was three hours later in New York. If she didn't call soon, the office would be closed for the day, and when her mom called she'd surely hear about it.

Cooper picked up the phone and dialed the number she had long-since memorized, having called it daily during her last two years of high school. After only one ring, Bob, a booker she didn't especially like, answered the phone.

"Yacomina Models," he said in his pushy way. After identifying herself, Cooper had to get through several of the nosy man's probing questions, before being passed on to her own booker.

"Well, it's about time, girl! We thought you fell of the face of the earth," Tara all but screamed into the phone.

"I know, I know," Cooper said, not exactly apologizing. "I've been really busy with school and everything."

"Oh, give me a break. You've been putting me off and you know it," Tara charged.

Cooper had almost forgotten that New York bluntness. In

Seattle, people were much less apt to say exactly what they were thinking and they were definitely too polite to call you on a little white lie like the one she had just told her booker. But Tara wasn't from Seattle, that was for sure. She was from Brooklyn and, like most New Yorkers, had a way of cutting right to the chase.

"So why have you been avoiding me?" she asked Cooper, point blank.

"I guess because I had no reason to call," Cooper said carefully. "I'm busy with school, like I said. And I'm not really looking to do any modeling. Besides, I'm all the way across the country. What do you want me to do, fly in for jobs?"

"Very funny, but you don't make enough yet to fly in for jobs. I was thinking more along the lines of that Seattle agency I asked you to call. I take it you haven't gotten around to that yet?"

Tara had accepted that Cooper wanted to go to college and was even accepting of her decision to attend school in Seattle, "although" she'd said, "you'd never catch me there." But Tara didn't see why Cooper couldn't model for a local agency while she went to school.

"Bella is a great agency, and their office is just a few blocks from your campus," Tara persisted. "I understand that you don't want to sign your life away, but why do you have to stop working altogether? Just give them a call."

"I'll think about it," Cooper said, noncommittally.

"Yeah. I know what that means. You're not going to call. Well are you at least coming back here for spring break? You have to promise me you'll drop by the office."

"Uh, not exactly. I'm going home with some friends to Oregon," Cooper admitted cautiously.

"Ore-gone! Why would you go to Ore-gone?" Tara's voice

was so loud Cooper had to hold the phone away from her ear. Even so, she couldn't help noticing how her booker pronounced the state's name in that East Coast way Ryan made fun of, with the emphasis on the last syllable.

"I thought it might be a nice change?" Cooper lamely volunteered.

"You've met some boy and he's poisoning your mind, isn't he?" Tara boomed. "Next thing you know, you'll be living in some little suburb with five kids and a body full of stretch marks. I won't be able to get you any work then!"

"Thanks for painting that flattering picture," Cooper laughed. "And yes I met someone, but he is not poisoning my mind! He's a great guy, and you'd really like him if you met him." Even as she spoke the words, though, Cooper wondered if they were true. She couldn't quite imagine Ryan and Tara in the same room together.

"Well then why don't you bring him to New York instead of running off to Ore-gone?" Tara asked.

"Because it's a lot more expensive to fly to New York. Besides, he invited me first. I don't know why I'm defending myself to you, anyway," Cooper told her.

"Look, that's fine. If you want to spend your spring vacation in the middle of nowhere rather than New York, be my guest. But promise me that if anything changes and you end up coming home after all, you'll stop by. You know, I'm not giving up on the idea of you going to Italy this summer. I've invested too much in you to just let you go."

"Sure, I'll let you know if anything changes." It was an easy promise to make; Cooper knew there was no way she'd be in New York next month.

After she hung up the phone she flopped down on her unmade bed. The call had been mentally draining. Cooper remembered all over again why she was glad to be away from New York and modeling. The way Tara made getting married and having babies and living in the suburbs sound like a fate worse than death was so typical. Sometimes Cooper thought that sort of life might be kind of nice, if she met the right guy.

She stretched on top of her rumpled down comforter and closed her eyes, trying to let all her thoughts and concerns melt away. No matter how hard she tried, though, her mind kept churning. When she did finally drift off, a million maybes haunted her dreams.

Maybe modeling is the only thing I'll ever be good at. Maybe I should have stayed in New York. Maybe I can't have a normal life. Maybe my mother was right....

After an hour or two of tossing and turning, the ringing phone finally pulled her from her sleep. Cooper quickly sat upright in bed, but it took her another minute to figure out where the sound was coming from before she groggily reached for the receiver.

"Hello?" she mumbled into the mouthpiece.

"Hi, darling, it's Mom."

"Oh, hi," Cooper responded. She tried to think of something more to say but her brain was still too fuzzy from sleep.

"Are you all right, dear? You sound like you just woke up. I bet all that rainy weather there is making you sick."

"No, Mom, I'm not sick," Cooper told her, exasperation creeping into her voice. "I sound like I just woke up because I *did* just wake up," she explained.

"Oh! Well, why are you sleeping in the middle of the day? Are you sure everything's okay?"

"Yeah, Mom. Everything's fine. I was just a little tired, so I took a nap before dinner."

"Well, okay. I wish I had time to lay around and do nothing

in the afternoons," her mom said, which Cooper took as a dig at her.

"Mom, I don't 'lay around in the afternoons.' I have a ton of studying to do tonight. I was just catching up on some lost sleep."

Sometimes Cooper felt like she and her mother connected on exactly the same wavelength, but at this moment, like at so many other moments, she felt like they were trains on two totally different tracks.

"Whatever, dear. Anyway, I didn't call to discuss your sleeping habits. I wanted to make sure you called Tara back. You know she's called here three times. I don't know why you can't just call and check in every now and then. I think she wants to know if you're going to Italy or not."

Cooper smiled at how well she had predicted her mother's actions. She was glad she had something to report.

"I talked to Tara just this afternoon, Mom." Cooper spoke nonchalantly, as if she spoke to her booker every afternoon.

"Oh, really?" her mom responded, a trace of skepticism in her voice.

"Yeah. She asked if I was coming home for spring break and I told her what my plans were. I promised that if anything changed and I was in New York, though, I would definitely stop by."

"Well that's something at least."

"But I won't be in New York, Mom," Cooper reminded her.

"I know, I know. I can't believe you'd choose some tiny town in Oregon over New York City, though."

"I just want to see where Ryan and Emily live. I thought it would be fun to try something new."

"I know," her mother relented finally, her voice softening. "And I do hope you have a good time, dear. But as your mother, I

43

can't help wishing you were coming home. You haven't been back to New York since you left for college. You spent Thanksgiving with Penny and Brian, and Christmas in Connecticut doesn't really count."

"You were the one who wanted to spend Christmas with Daddy's family out in Connecticut instead of staying in New York. I came home for Christmas; home just happened to be Grandma and Grandpa Ellis's this year."

"I know, that was my decision. But it doesn't change the fact that you still haven't been back to the City since leaving for college. Don't you miss it?"

Cooper thought for a moment. She did miss certain things about New York. There were always a million things to do, and she just had to walk out her door and there were three markets, five restaurants, two newsstands and a movie theater all within two blocks. Seattle didn't have quite that variety.

"Well, don't you?" her mom prompted. "I know I could never be away from this city for longer than a month at a time. I'd go crazy."

"But I'm not you, Mom. Maybe New York just isn't my home anymore," Cooper said.

"I know you're not me, Cooper. But New York *is* your home, even though you may wish it were otherwise right now," her mom insisted. "You're going to grow and change, but this will always be your home. You have so many memories here and I believe that someday you'll realize you like it more than you've been willing to admit."

Cooper just sighed loudly into the phone.

"I heard that," her mom said. "And I know you think I don't understand you," she continued. "As hard as it is to believe, I was eighteen once, too. I know you want to experience new places and things right now, so go ahead. You try on other people's lives for a while, but eventually you'll find your own skin still fits best."

"Thank you for that nice little story, Mom," Cooper laughed. "That means you're fine with me going to Ore-gone, I guess?" she asked, purposely mispronouncing it.

"Yes, and I hope you have a wonderful time, honey, I really do. But know that we miss you and that you are expected to spend every vacation for the rest of your life with your parents," her mom joked.

"Dream on," Cooper laughed, then added more seriously, "I miss you, too, Mom." Her mother could get to her like no one else, but she was still her mother.

"Oh, and one last thing, dear," her mom said. "You're still keeping an open mind about going to Italy this summer aren't you?"

"Good-bye, Mother," was Cooper's response. "Tell Daddy I said hello and I'll e-mail him this week."

"Good-bye, sweetheart."

The first half of the week seemed to drag on forever as Cooper looked forward to her big anniversary celebration with Ryan on Wednesday. Then, just when she thought the night would never arrive, it did.

For the event, she wore her favorite dress, which was black and sleeveless, ending just above her knee. She wore strappy black sandals on her feet and the palest pastel blue hose that went with her nail polish. She and Claire had found the polish at a drugstore in downtown New York and between them they had collected every shade. Emily said it made her fingernails look like those candy-coated almonds people gave out at weddings, but Cooper didn't care. She decided the look was perfect and she was glad the dress still fit after six months of the cafeteria's starchy meals.

Once she was dressed, Cooper set about putting the final touches on her make-up. She knew Ryan really liked a more natural look, so she tried to just play up her features and left her hair down instead of in the twist she usually wore with that dress. Even so, she couldn't resist adding a bit of lipstick in a shimmery pastel shade that complimented her fingers and toes perfectly. She checked the dainty rhinestone clip that fastened her bangs over to one side and sprayed a little perfume on her hair before stepping back to get the full effect.

She had to admit she was pleased with the final result, which was saying a lot. Even after several years of modeling Cooper still felt awkward and gangly. Compliments about her looks only made her uncomfortable. She knew she had just as many flaws as anyone else—her feet were big, her nose was slightly crooked, her arms were way too skinny. But she was never able to voice her feelings of inadequacy, knowing that when "pretty" girls complain, it's seen as whining or as if they're fishing for more compliments, and neither trait helped to win friends. It was like trying to explain why she didn't want to model. There was no way to say it without being mistaken for just another beautiful woman complaining about the trials of beauty. Cooper couldn't help feeling a little misunderstood.

The sound of Kenzie opening the suite door to let Ryan in brought Cooper out of her reverie. She grabbed a little black purse off her bed and threw the lipstick inside, along with her keys and a little bit of cash. When she entered the other room Ryan was waiting there alone, Kenzie apparently having gone back into her own room. He sat perched on the edge of the ugly avocado couch that was one of the room's only pieces of furniture.

"You look great," Ryan said, rising to give her a "hello" kiss.

As she pulled away a moment later, Cooper took in her boyfriend's khaki pants and neatly pressed denim shirt.

"You don't look so bad yourself, Mr. Stewart. And no base-ball hat. This is a special occasion!"

"Oh, uh, thanks," he mumbled, smoothing down the front of his shirt.

As they walked toward the car Cooper noticed that Ryan seemed nervous. She thought it was kind of cute that after all this time dating, there was still some excitement. She was glad they weren't so familiar they knew each other's every move. Just as they approached the truck, Ryan turned to her as if to block her path. Cooper looked up at him questioningly.

"I have to tell you something," he blurted out, but it was already too late. She looked over his shoulder to where the truck was parked. There in the cab sat Drew, a friend of theirs who lived in Ryan's dorm. When she caught his eye he gave her a smile. Cooper just stared, then numbly waved.

"You invited Drew along on our anniversary dinner?" she asked, her voice rising with each word.

"Just let me explain," Ryan pleaded.

"What is there to explain? It's a yes or no question."

"Okay, then, I guess it's yes," Ryan admitted, then hastily added, "but there were extenuating circumstances."

Cooper couldn't believe it. She thought he was nervous because of her, but he was really just afraid to tell her that he had invited Drew along on their special night! This was just too much.

"Cooooo-per, will you just listen to me?" Ryan asked. She hated when he said her name in the long drawn-out way that meant he thought she was being unreasonable. Why could he always make her feel like she was in the wrong? He was the one who had invited someone else along on their date. And it wasn't like it was just any date. Tonight was supposed to be special. Still, she decided, she might as well hear what he had to say. Cooper turned back to Ryan, an expectant look on her face.

"Okay, now just listen to me," Ryan said, then proceeded to make his case. "Drew stopped by earlier and he was really depressed. You remember, he's dated that one girl, Kelly, a few times? Well, he just found out she had a boyfriend back home that she failed to mention. I felt like he needed a friend tonight, so I made him come along."

"I understand you wanted to be a good friend, but Dan and Emily and Kenzie and Chris are all at The Cup & Chaucer. It's not like he'd be spending the night alone in his room if you didn't invite him along," Cooper pointed out.

"That's true, but I think he just feels more comfortable talking to me...I mean to us. Won't you just give it a chance? The longer we stand out here talking about it the more he's going to think you don't want him to come."

Cooper felt trapped.

"Oh, great! So now I end up being the jerk because I want to be alone with you on our anniversary," Cooper exclaimed.

"I don't know what the big deal is. Our friend needs us! And he doesn't know it's our anniversary. Besides, we can celebrate some other time. I'll take you out for Ground Hog Day or something," Ryan offered.

Cooper had to struggle to keep her voice under control. "Ground Hog Day just passed and you know that's not the same thing. But I don't want Drew to feel bad, so let's just go get in the truck and go to dinner."

"Fine with me. And by the way, you're gonna love the restaurant I picked," he told her enthusiastically.

"I can barely wait."

There was still tension in the air as Cooper slid in next to Drew. It wasn't until after seat belts were fastened and Ryan turned the key in the ignition that the silence was broken.

"You know you can just drop me at The Cup," Drew said, more to Cooper than Ryan. "I don't want to ruin your night."

Cooper's expression softened. She knew it wasn't Drew's fault.

"Don't worry about it," She told him, smiling warmly. "It's no big deal."

That seemed to be all the reassurance either guy needed.

"So do you think PCU will make it to the playoffs this year?" Drew asked Ryan, and the conversation centered around sports the rest of the way to the restaurant. Then, just as Ryan announced "this is it," he made a sharp turn into a parking lot, throwing Cooper almost into Drew's lap.

"Cooper, I didn't know you felt that way about me," Drew joked.

She felt her cheeks turn bright red and it took her several seconds to untangle herself. When she finally did she peered out the windshield at the waterfront. There were buildings all along the shore but they were parked directly in front of Ivar's Acres of Clams.

"Tell me that's not where we're eating," Cooper said, pointing to the restaurant with a picture of an old weathered fisherman out front.

"Of course not," Ryan answered, sounding offended. "Not that there's anything wrong with Ivar's, though. They have great clam chowder as a matter of fact."

As they crossed the street Cooper glanced up at the menu board in front of the restaurant.

"They also sell clam *nectar*," she pointed out. "Isn't that great, too?"

"I refuse to answer that question on the grounds that it might incriminate me," Ryan told her. A few steps further down they walked under a pretend street sign that said "Clam Central Station." *Oh, that is so cheesy!* she thought, but chose to keep her further criticisms of Ivar's fine establishment to herself.

With an arm around her shoulder, Ryan steered her into another building a few yards down while Drew followed behind. Cooper didn't lean into Ryan the way she usually did or make any move to put her arm around his waist like she might under other circumstances. Ryan wasn't off the hook just yet.

Inside they found the entrances to several shops, as well as a restaurant called The Crab Pot. It certainly wasn't a romantic *sounding* restaurant, but Cooper cautioned herself to give it a chance.

Ryan told the hostess the number of people in their party and luckily they were seated right away. It was a cute place, with the expected nautical decor, and Cooper relaxed a little as she took her seat. They could still have a very nice anniversary dinner, she decided, allowing her anger to dissipate a little. As a gesture of good will she smiled across the table at Ryan before looking down at her menu.

Cooper had just about decided on the crab salad when their waitress appeared.

"Hi, how are you guys doing tonight?" she asked in that way waitresses do without really expecting an answer.

Everyone looked up at her, waiting for her to continue.

"Have you been to The Crab Pot before?" she asked the group.

They all shook their heads "no."

"Then let me tell you about our sea feasts. You just have to try them. What we do is bring you a huge bucket of fresh seafood steamed in our mouth-watering spice mixture, along with corn on the cob, red potatoes, and Cajun sausage. Then we dump it out on the table, give you each a mallet, and let you have at it. It's a ton of food and very popular."

Both Ryan's and Drew's eyes lit up at that. Cooper just sort of shook her head. Any other time she would have thought it sounded like fun, but it was their anniversary and she was all dressed up. They didn't really expect her to eat with her fingers, did they?

Apparently they did.

"C'mon Cooper, it sounds great," Ryan coaxed. "And we can get the one with crab or mussels or salmon."

Cooper was still skeptical.

"Look, I even have a coupon for it," Ryan said proudly, pulling a crumpled piece of paper from his pants pocket.

Cooper leaned forward to read it. Sure enough, it was a two-for-one coupon good on any of The Crab Pot's sea feasts. For some inexplicable reason, she almost burst into tears right there at the table. Didn't Ryan understand this night was supposed to be special? There was nothing wrong with using coupons. In fact, the girls were always collecting them for frozen yogurt and pizza delivery. They would have to eat all their meals in the cafeteria if it weren't for these discounts, but still....

Cooper looked up to find both guys looking at her expectantly. It was obviously two against one. For a moment, she considered getting a salad and letting them order the sea feast alone, but she knew it wouldn't be the same.

"All right," she finally agreed. "But I want the one with the two different kinds of crab."

"You're on," Ryan told her, before ordering drinks for the group.

Their waitress soon returned and began tying big plastic bibs around each of their necks. Cooper started to protest, but knew it wouldn't do any good. Their table was then covered with butcher paper and a small cutting board, and little wooden mallets were placed in front of each of them. Surrendering the fantasy of a romantic anniversary dinner once and for all, Cooper leaned back in her seat and began tapping her single utensil rhythmically against the table while the boys busied themselves with trying to smash each other's fingers with theirs.

Soon enough it was time to eat, and a huge metal bowl of food was unceremoniously deposited in the middle of their table. Ryan and Drew dug in quickly, while Cooper was a bit more hesitant. Eventually, though, she reached in and plucked out a few mussels and two tender red potato halves from the pile.

"Cooper, you have to try the shrimp," Ryan told her, handing her one. It was still in its shell so she removed it as delicately as possible, pulling off the tail before popping it in her mouth.

Just as Cooper was about to admit that it was indeed pretty good, Ryan cracked into one of the crab halves and juice went spurting across the table, hitting her right in the eye. She tried to wipe the liquid from her face, but her hands were a mess. When she raised a finger to her eye it only made things worse, and the spices from her hands caused tears to stream down her face. She dabbed at them with a dirty corner of her napkin, but that didn't help either.

The boys were so busy eating they didn't even notice. Finally, she excused herself and went to find a bathroom. It turned out she had to walk outside and around the building, then go back in. By the time she washed her hands, wiped all the excess mascara from under her eyes, and made her way back to the table, Ryan and Drew were leaning back in their chairs with satisfied smiles on their faces.

"What took you so long?" Ryan asked. "Are you alright?"

"I'm fine. I just had something in my eye."

"Oh yeah, I can tell. Your right eye's all bloodshot," Ryan pointed out after examining Cooper more closely.

She ate the crab leg she had left at her place, but when she finished that one and was ready for another she noticed there weren't any left. She found two shrimp under a pile of empty mussel shells and ate several pieces of sausage, but she was really in the mood for crab. After a few more pieces of potato she joined the boys by removing her bib and leaning back in her chair, too.

"Did you get enough to eat? How about some corn?" Ryan asked, holding out a small cob.

"No, I'm fine, thanks."

As soon as the words were out of her mouth their waitress was standing next to their table again.

"Can I clear this away for you?"

"Please," Cooper all but pleaded, because their table looked like a war zone. Their waitress had obviously had lots of practice, though. She quickly gathered the corners of the butcher paper together and whisked away the entire mess, then set their bill on the newly clean table.

"I'll take that when you're ready."

On the drive home, Cooper got to sit next to Ryan, but by then it was too late. The evening was ruined. And just when she was positive there was nothing that could make her feel any worse about the evening, Ryan pulled up in front of her dorm and just sat there with the truck idling. Before it could even sink in that he wasn't planning on walking her to her door, Drew quickly hopped out of the passenger side and let her out. Cooper thanked Ryan politely for the dinner, and turned to go into her dorm. When she turned to wave one last time, Ryan had already driven off.

Once inside her dorm room, Cooper saw the card and small gift-wrapped package she had planned to give Ryan when he brought her home that night. Inside were two tickets to a Seattle Supersonics game, but her gift was just one more part of the evening that had been ruined.

It was stupid of me to get Ryan an anniversary present or even to bring the whole thing up at all. It certainly didn't mean anything to him. Wallowing in a puddle of self-pity, she threw the unwrapped tickets and unopened card into her desk drawer.

As Cooper was slipping her pajamas over her head, Emily burst into the room. Obviously on a sugar high from drinking too many hot chocolates, she gushed about the picture Dan had drawn of her on a napkin at The Cup & Chaucer that night. As she stuck the likeness up on her bulletin board Cooper tried to think of what she would say when Emily asked about her evening. She was still preparing her answer when the questions began.

"You're home kind of early, aren't you?" Em asked innocently enough.

"I guess," Cooper answered evasively.

"Well, did you have a nice anniversary?"

"Oh, sure. It was—" Cooper began, but then couldn't finish her sentence. She couldn't quite spit out the word "nice." She paused for a minute, then looked at her roommate and spilled the whole story.

"That is just like that dumb brother of mine," Emily sympathized. "He's about as romantic as a rock, but if it helps any, I know he really likes you."

"Thanks, but I'm not so sure of that after tonight."

"Oh, no. He does. He's just so much like our father, though. Dad's always running out in the middle of dinner or on his day off to meet with someone who's depressed or upset and just needs to talk with a pastor."

"And your mom's okay with that?" Cooper asked, incredulous.

"They worked out a system a long time ago. He never commits to something or breaks a date with his family without talking to her about it first, and she has veto power. That way she can always say, 'Hey, you've been gone five out of the last six nights. Can that person's problem keep until the morning?' instead of just letting him go and then being all upset about it."

"That was all I wanted!" Cooper exclaimed. "If he had just called and asked my opinion before inviting Drew along, or at least given me a little warning, I would have been fine. But sometimes I think my feelings matter less to him than anyone else's."

"In some ways they probably do...I mean, as far as how much he takes them into account. It's not that Ryan doesn't care about your feelings, but he just assumes you'll understand because he would if the situation were reversed," Emily explained.

"But the situation would never be reversed! I would never have invited, say for instance, *you* along on our anniversary dinner. No offense intended."

"Exactly. But he just can't seem to understand that everyone doesn't think and react to situations exactly the same way he does. And no offense taken, thank you," Emily said, smiling.

"I don't know what I'm going to do," Cooper concluded.

"I don't know what to tell you," Emily said. "He's my brother and I love him, but I could never date someone like him, that's for sure. I think you should be nominated for sainthood."

"I'd hold off on the ceremony just yet," Cooper advised, "but thanks. It feels better just to have talked about it and to know that it's not just me overreacting. It really was an awful night."

"It sure sounds like it," Emily agreed. "Why don't you just go to sleep? Try not to dream of giant, man-eating clams."

"I think I'll do that," Cooper told her, crawling under the covers and turning off her light. But as she pulled her blankets under her chin she could still smell the strong scent of seafood on her fingers.

7

ooper was lost in thought as she crossed campus, heading for The Snack Shop and a strawberry fruit shake, when she ran into Brian.

"Hey there, my almost-uncle. How's it going? You teaching a class today?"

"Yes, and that's Mr. Almost-Uncle to you," he teased.

"Oh, sorry. I'll be certain to afford you the respect you deserve from now on, sir," she tossed back.

"Where are you headed?"

"The Snack Shop," Cooper answered. "You want to join me?"

"Sure, I've got some time, and I was just going to spend it grading papers," he explained.

"That might be more fun than an hour with me," Cooper told him.

"Why, what's up?"

"Nothing much," she said unconvincingly.

"It sounds like you need to talk," Brian observed. "Here, have a seat in this booth and I'll go get our food. What do you want?"

"Just a fruit shake, thanks," Cooper said, then called out after him, "a strawberry-banana one, please!"

A few minutes later, Brian came back and placed in front of Cooper a big paper cup with milkshake dripping down the sides.

"So what is it? Guy trouble?" Brian asked.

"How'd you guess?" Cooper said, laying her head down on the table dramatically. Then looking back up at Brian, she added, "I don't know. Maybe it's just me."

"You and Ryan having problems?"

"I think Ryan's fine," Cooper told him. "It's just me who's having the problems."

"What did he do?" Brian asked, sounding like a protective father.

"Nothing," Cooper told him. "It's nothing really."

"If it were nothing, I don't think you'd be so upset. What's up?"

"Well it's a lot of little things culminating in one big thing last night."

"Do you want to tell me about any of these things, or would you rather not talk to a guy about it?" Brian asked.

"Actually, I think a guy's opinion is just what I need," Cooper told him. "I can't tell if I'm overreacting or if I really have a reason to be upset. It might help to get an impartial opinion."

"Fire away, then."

Cooper repeated her story of The Crab Pot fiasco, then added details about the other little problems she and Ryan had been having lately, trying to be as fair as possible in the retelling of it all.

"Well, I can definitely see why you're upset," Brian said. "Penny would strangle me if I did that on our anniversary. But you know, in all fairness to Ryan, it took me awhile to understand that. I did some really insensitive things when Penny and I were first dating."

"Like what?" Cooper asked, leaning forward with interest.

"Like believing her when she said it was all right if I wanted to go to a football game with some old college friends on the day she got her wisdom teeth out. As she explained later, she wanted *me* to make the decision to be there for her. She didn't want to have to *tell* me it was the right thing to do. Now, for any medical procedure, big or small, I'm in the waiting room. But I learned that one the hard way."

"Yeah," Cooper agreed. "I'd like to think if I were having an appendectomy or something Ryan would be there for me, but I'm not sure."

"Look, I'm the first to admit guys can be pretty selfish sometimes. You have to knock us over the head every now and then, but most of us do get it eventually," Brian said. "So there is hope."

"I don't know if I can hang in there until eventually," Cooper told him. She was beginning to consider the possibility that maybe things weren't going to work out with Ryan after all.

"I'm not so worried about you working through this anniversary thing. I think if you sit down with Ryan and explain how you feel, just like you did right now with me, he'll understand. You just wanted to be in on the decision and to know that your feelings matter, too. What concerns me, though, is all the little stuff."

Cooper wasn't quite sure what he meant. She'd been putting up with the little stuff for six months and was sure she could continue to deal with it. It was the anniversary dinner that had really set her off. That was the big issue as far as she was concerned.

"You keep saying this relationship is what you want," Brian continued, "but I think you have to ask yourself why."

"What do you mean why? Ryan's a great guy, he's a strong Christian, and we have fun together," Cooper pointed out.

"Look, I'm not saying Ryan isn't a great guy, but are you sure he's the *right* great guy for you? There's nothing wrong with admitting that things just aren't working out. That's the point of dating: to try out different relationships and find what makes you happy."

"But Ryan does make me happy!" Cooper insisted. "We can sit and talk for hours over a single cup of coffee about the littlest things, and I trust him more than any other guy I know. He always makes me feel so safe and like he's looking out for me."

"Then I guess you need to weigh how important it is to you that he share your interests. If he doesn't do the things you like with you now, that's probably not going to change down the road. And if you don't enjoy hiking and camping and sitting in the bleachers at his basketball games now, how are you going to feel after spending the next four years doing just that...or the next forty years, for that matter?"

"But you and Penny don't do everything together! You always complain when she drags you along shopping, and she hates it when you watch college football for hours on end."

"That's true. We don't like all the same things. That would be boring. The difference is, we have enough important things in common that if I spend a Saturday afternoon watching a college game with my friends it's not a big deal. I don't force her to come along, and when we meet up again we have something to talk about."

"I think Ryan and I have enough important stuff in common," Cooper said. "We just need to work on things a little."

"Okay, if you're sure. You know I'm not trying to tell you to break up. And I know it's none of my business, anyway. I just don't like to see you so unhappy. It's true, relationships are hard work and I admire you for not just giving up when things are tough. But I don't know if you should have to work quite so hard."

"Oh, I don't mind, really," Cooper insisted, but she had to admit it had been nicer in the beginning when everything was easy.

"Does Ryan mind?" Brian asked, "or even notice? You want to make sure you're not the one who's always compromising, because that won't work. You'll just get resentful."

"You're right. And I promise, I'm going to talk to Ryan about that and about last night. We won't really have time until after the game Saturday night. The coach has been working them like crazy. But I will bring it up. And thanks for letting me cry on your shoulder. Aunt Penny's lucky to have you, even with your college football addiction and lack of culinary skills."

"Thanks for the compliment...I think."

They both laughed and Cooper couldn't believe how much better she felt.

Cooper glanced at her watch just then and realized they had been talking for over an hour.

"Oh, my gosh, I'm missing my chemistry lab! I have to go!"

She gave Brian a quick hug and thanked him again for the fruit shake and the advice before racing across campus to the science building. As she breathlessly took her seat at one of the workstations, she glanced up at the clock above the chalkboard. She was ten minutes late. That was another thing she and Ryan argued about: he was always right on time and Cooper, no matter how early she started getting ready, was always running a few minutes behind. *Well, that's just one more area I'll have to work on,* she resolved.

Later that afternoon, upon entering her suite, Cooper found Kenzie and Chris rehearsing in the living room while their friend Allie looked on.

"Hey, Cooper!" Allie called out. "You're just in time for the big concert. C'mon over here, I can get you front row seats," she said, patting the spot next to her on the ugly green couch. When Cooper joined her, Allie leaned over and whispered loudly, "I'm a close personal friend of the artists you know," then winked with great exaggeration. Cooper couldn't help laughing.

Cooper spent over an hour listening to the duo play, while Allie shouted out requests like a crazed groupie. During a break between songs Kenzie disappeared into her room, only to return with a towel draped around her neck like a scarf. She resumed playing, then whipped the towel off, tossing it into the "audience" where Allie caught it and squealed loudly, the way fans used to react to Elvis when he did the same thing.

"But where's your white jumpsuit?" Cooper called to Kenzie, causing her to launch into an impromptu Elvis medley, with Chris doing a fair imitation of the King, for a blond. Never one to sit still for very long, Allie jumped to her feet, pulled Cooper up off the couch, and spun her around several times in a clumsy jitterbug. Soon they were all dancing around the suite, singing loudly.

As the last strains of "Hound Dog" faded away, they all collapsed onto the couch together, laughing and out of breath, while Allie sprawled across Kenzie and Cooper's laps.

"Remind me never to invite you to another rehearsal," Kenzie told Allie, giving her a friendly push that rolled her onto the floor. "You're very disruptive," she added with mock disapproval.

"I invited myself, thank you very much," an indignant Allie

shot back, getting to her feet and brushing herself off. "And you'd better watch it since I plan to be in the audience, front and center, every time you two play. Need I remind you that this afternoon's little performance can easily be repeated?"

"You wouldn't dare," Kenzie threatened while Chris and Cooper exchanged alarmed looks. There was no doubt in Cooper's mind that Allie would get up and dance on the table at Kenzie and Chris' big debut if she felt like it.

"I wouldn't push her if I were you," Cooper interjected.

"Maybe you're right," Kenzie relented then turned to Allie. "Okay, you can come to rehearsal anytime you want, but please promise me you won't embarrass me when we play in front of other people. I'll already be nervous enough."

"Okay, it's a deal," Allie agreed.

"I guess that's it for today then," Chris said, stowing his guitar in its case. "I better hit the books for a while before dinner."

"Yeah, and I've got a five-page paper due in the morning that I haven't even started yet," Allie groaned, following Chris to the door.

"Jhall vee meet up at Chèz PCU for deenair at ahround zeex o'clock?" Allie proposed in a fake French accent.

"Wee-wee, mad-uh-mo-say-ell," Kenzie replied, foregoing a French accent for an exaggerated version of her Southern drawl.

"Count me in, too," Cooper said as Chris and Allie were leaving.

When they were alone in the suite Cooper followed Kenzie into her room.

"So are all your rehearsals so much fun?" she asked. "'Cuz if they are, I might have to start showing up more often."

"They're usually a little tamer than this, but I enjoy 'em," Kenzie answered.

"And that enjoyment wouldn't have anything to do with who you're playing with, now would it?" Cooper teased.

"I can't imagine what you're talking about," Kenzie replied innocently, but then she broke into a dimpled smile.

"Mm-hmm. I thought so!"

"Okay, you caught me, but isn't he just so cute? And then when he starts singing I can't help it; I *melt*. Which is so dumb—I've been around musicians my whole life, for cryin' out loud!" Kenzie lamented. Then with a note of disgust in her voice she added, "Oh, man, I'm so mushy, it's hurl-worthy."

"Yep, you sure are," Cooper laughed, nodding her agreement. "How are you going to manage over spring break when you don't see him for a whole week?"

"I'll just have to suffer through, I guess," Kenzie said. "At least I know we'll most likely be spending half the summer together."

"What do you mean?" Cooper looked at her in surprise. "Where are you going? More importantly, why wasn't I invited?"

Kenzie laughed. "It looks like Chris and I will both be on staff at Malibu this summer."

"That Young Life camp in Canada where you met him and Allie?"

"That's the one," Kenzie said. "Sorry, Coop. Only Young Lifers allowed. Maybe next year, though, if you become a leader."

"I don't know," Cooper replied. "I always wanted to go to camp when I was younger, but I'm not sure about the whole counselor thing."

But even as the last words were still coming out of her mouth Cooper could tell Kenzie wasn't listening anymore. She was already planning all the fun she was going to have with Chris.

On Saturday morning Cooper stopped off at The Perfect Bagel on her way to the Seattle Art Museum. She had told Ryan she wouldn't ask him to go with her if he took her out for their anniversary, so she was going alone...even though she questioned whether he had really kept his part of the bargain. Anyway, he had a game that night and Cooper knew he would want to stick around campus and rest up. They never did much on game days.

Spending the day apart didn't make them incompatible, Cooper tried to convince herself. She had to admit, though, the thought of sitting through another basketball game that night wasn't all that appealing, even if Ryan was playing.

Cooper swung open the door to the bagel shop and saw Sam instantly this time. Still feeling a twinge of guilt over their last conversation, she made an effort to be more friendly.

"Hey, Sam. Do you live here or what?" she asked as she approached the newspaper-strewn table where he was sitting.

He glanced up and it was hard to mistake the look of surprise on his face. This was the first time Cooper had ever initiated a conversation with him, and he obviously wasn't sure how to take it.

Determined to be nice, Cooper tried again.

"Is that a Sunday *New York Times* you're reading?" pointing at the fat paper stacked in front of him.

Finally Sam seemed to recover from the shock.

"Uh, yeah, it is," he offered lamely.

"But today's Saturday. How'd you get it?"

"It's last Sunday's. A friend of mine works at that little newsstand on Broadway. If all the papers haven't sold out by midweek, he gives me a free copy. His boss said it's all right because they'd just end up in the trash."

"That's cool," Cooper said, eyeing the Arts & Entertainment section peeking out from under the front page.

"You want to read a section?" Sam offered. "I'm done with all of these." He gestured to a stack on the seat next to him.

"Oh, no. But thanks anyway. I'm going to the Seattle Art Museum. I just stopped off for a little breakfast first," Cooper explained. She really did want a look at the paper—she used to love reading it, especially on the weekends when she and her parents spread out in the living room and passed the sections back and forth between them—but she didn't want to admit that to Sam.

He shrugged his shoulders as if to say, "your loss," then began offering museum tips to Cooper.

"I love the Seattle Art Museum," Sam enthused. "I spent hours there the first time I went and have been back twice since. You really need to go to the Frye, though, too. They have a Manet and a Mary Cassatt that I thought were interesting."

Now it was Cooper's turn to be shocked. "You like museums?" she asked.

"Yeah, I was the one kid in elementary school who really enjoyed those field trips not because we got out of class, but because I loved the art we saw there."

"I always loved those field trips, too! My friend Claire calls me a 'museum geek,' but I don't care."

"Don't you miss the Met?" Sam asked.

Cooper nodded. She loved New York's Metropolitan Museum of Art. "Yeah, but I won't be going back anytime soon."

"Well on your tour of Seattle's art treasures you have to go to the Toaster Museum."

"The Toaster Museum?" Cooper repeated. "You're making that up!"

"No, I promise, it really exists," Sam vowed, raising two fingers in a Boy Scout salute.

"Oh, my friend Alex would love that. I'll have to tell him about it."

After that there was an awkward pause before Cooper broke the silence.

"I guess I better go put in my order or I'll never make it to the museum."

"Yeah, I suppose you should," Sam agreed.

"Well, bye then."

"See you later," Sam said before looking back down at his paper.

Being nice to Sam wasn't so hard after all, Cooper reluctantly admitted to herself as she crunched into her bagel. *Even if we did talk about New York. In fact, he was pretty interesting.*

At the game later that night the noise from the crowd in the gym was deafening, and Cooper had to cover her ears as she, Emily, and Dan made their way up into the stands. It was already the middle of the first period when they sat down next to a bunch of guys with their faces painted blue and gold. On the other side, a group of girls waved pom-poms in the air and squealed for a player named Scott. Cooper tried to get into the game, studying the scoreboard during time-outs and following Ryan with her eyes the rest of the time.

Cooper had never watched an entire basketball game until she came to PCU, so it was still a little difficult for her to understand what was going on at any given moment. Ryan had been very patient about teaching her, though, and really wanted her to love the game the way he did. His enthusiasm was contagious, but she had to admit she would still rather read a good book. She was glad sports hadn't been a big deal at her high school.

Cooper wouldn't have minded so much if the whole crowd didn't have to stand every time PCU scored, but they did. Every few minutes she was forced up from her seat by the sheer force of the people around her.

"You want some popcorn?" Emily offered, holding a bag out toward her roommate. Just as Cooper started to say "no, thank you," PCU scored and the crowd rose to its feet for what Cooper was sure was the millionth time. In the process, the bag of popcorn got knocked out of Emily's hands and flew through the air, raining kernels down on the two girls' heads.

"If you didn't want any popcorn you could have just said so," Emily laughed, picking pieces out of Cooper's hair.

Ryan did manage to score three times, causing Cooper to cheer loudly. Aside from that, the game was uneventful, with PCU soundly trampling the other team whose name Cooper had forgotten by the time they filed back down the bleachers.

Since Ryan still had to shower, they decided to meet him over at The Cup & Chaucer. Cooper felt more relaxed once they were there, in their usual table near the back where Drew, Ethan, and Allie waited, having left the game early to save everyone seats. The coffeehouse scene was definitely more

Cooper's thing, but sometimes she was surprised that Ryan liked it as much as he did. Tonight would be especially fun, because Kenzie and Chris were playing for the first time. Kenzie said they had really improved since that night Cooper listened to them rehearse.

She was on her second mocha latté when Ryan arrived. Chris and Kenzie had just been introduced, and Cooper leaned over and gave Ryan a kiss on the cheek before whispering "good game" into his ear. Ryan thanked her then turned his attention to the stage where their friends were playing a soft ballad-like tune. Suddenly Cooper had a funny feeling in the pit of her stomach. Ryan hadn't said anything, but somehow she sensed something was wrong. She tried to push the feeling aside, but it kept returning.

Finally Cooper couldn't stand it anymore. Maybe she was just being silly, but she needed to put her fears to rest once and for all. She leaned over to Ryan again.

"Is everything all right?"

He turned to look at her and just when she was sure he was going to dismiss her suspicions, he blurted out, "As a matter of fact it isn't. Do you think we could get out of here and go somewhere a little more private? I really need to talk to you."

"Sure," Cooper agreed, grabbing her black leather jacket from the back of her chair and slipping her arms into the sleeves. They quickly said their good-byes and headed for the door. She would have to apologize to Kenzie later for missing the rest of the show, but it must be important for Ryan to look so serious.

Cooper was still trying to figure out what Ryan could be so upset about as she climbed up into the passenger seat of his truck.

"Did something happen after the game tonight?" she asked,

her voice filled with concern. "Was someone kicked off the team?"

"No, it's nothing like that," Ryan told her.

"Then what's up? You're starting to scare me a little."

He continued to put her off until they pulled in front of her dorm. Only after removing the keys from the ignition did Ryan finally turn to Cooper and begin talking.

"I'm sorry if I scared you. It has nothing to do with the game tonight."

"Well then what are you so upset about?" Cooper asked. She was completely mystified by his behavior. His next words made things clearer than she wanted them to, however.

"It's about us," he said, the words catching in his throat. "This is really hard for me to say, but I just don't know how to make it work anymore."

Cooper stared at him. She felt like she had been physically punched. "So what are you saying, that you want to break up?" she asked, barely able to get the words past her throat.

"I'm not saying I want to. I'm saying we should."

"Why, just because we have a few problems we need to work through? You're just going to dump me?"

"I'm not dumping you," Ryan insisted.

"Then we're not breaking up?" Cooper asked, forcing back the tears that threatened to spill down her cheeks.

"Cooper, this is hard on me, too, but do you really think we should stay together?"

"But it's not fair!" Cooper wailed, letting out just a bit of the emotion that was bubbling to the surface. "I've tried so hard to be just what you wanted."

"That's part of the problem," Ryan said. "I'm not saying it's your fault, but I don't want you to be something you're not for me and I don't want to have to be something I'm not."

"But everyone has to compromise in relationships," Cooper pointed out. "Why can't we work through this?"

"Because I don't think we can change who we are, and if we keep dating I'm afraid we'll end up not liking each other very much."

"This is about the other night, isn't it?" Cooper said, spitting the accusation at Ryan. "You're mad because I didn't want Drew to come along on our anniversary dinner."

"I'm not mad at you about that. You were the one who was upset, and you probably had a right to be. But if I had the night to do over again I have to say I would make the same decisions."

"That's nice to know," Cooper said sarcastically. She really wanted to hear that he was sorry, that the six months they had spent together meant something to him, too.

"Look Cooper, you deserve someone who is going to remember things like six-month anniversaries, because that's important to you. You deserve someone who will go to museums with you and not spend the whole time asking when he can leave."

"But I don't want those things, I want you," Cooper tried to explain, but Ryan just shook his head.

"Look, I know you probably won't believe me, but this is tearing me up, too. I promise you, the last thing I ever wanted to do was hurt you, but I don't think I'm going to change my mind about this. It's for the best."

For the best. How many times had Cooper heard that before? Who did he think he was, her parents? She knew she should be mature and continue to calmly try to change his mind, but at that moment she just wanted to hurt Ryan like he was hurting her. She knew he hated it when she walked away from a discussion—Ryan was really big on resolving things—so she hopped out of the truck, said "thanks for the ride home," and slammed the door on any further conversation.

The victory was short-lived, though. Once inside her dorm room Cooper let the tears flow, crying for so long she was afraid she would never be able to stop. Finally, with a few gulping sobs, she pulled herself together. Then she cranked up her stereo, grabbed her computer and plugged in her modem. She wasn't really ready to talk to anyone yet, but at least she could vent to Claire and Alex via the Internet. They would sympathize with her and tell her that that jerk Ryan didn't deserve her anyway. Even if she didn't believe it, that was what she needed to hear at that moment.

Cooper logged on and was glad to find a message from Alex in her e-mail box. She clicked the "read" button on her screen and started scanning the message.

> Hi, Coop! It's both of us, Claire and Alex, coming to you from Alex's apartment. We have some big news and since you're not coming home for spring break we decided we'd just have to tell you this way. Are you curious yet? Well, you'll never guess so we'll tell you. Go ahead, Claire. No, no, you do it, Alex. Okay, we'll both do it: WE'RE IN LOVE! We know, we know, it seems unbelievable, but it's true. And we're sickeningly happy so maybe it's better you're not coming home. We don't know if you could stand to be around us right now. Call one of us this week and we'll give you all the juicy details, until then...
> Love, Peace & Plenty of Quarters to do Your Laundry,
> Alex & Claire

Cooper switched off her computer without even closing out of the application. She couldn't believe this. *God, this is a joke, right?* she asked, looking up at the ceiling and waiting for a divine answer. During high school she and Claire had often discussed the possibility of one or the other of them dating Alex, but both agreed they could never do it. He was so much fun and definitely cute, but neither of them liked him in "that way." He was like a brother. Obviously, Claire had changed her mind. *Well, she picked a fine time to do it,* Cooper thought angrily.

Emily would be home soon and Cooper wasn't ready to face any questions so she quickly got ready for bed and turned the light out. Of course, she couldn't fall asleep, but she lay there with her eyes closed. In twenty minutes or so, Emily came in, assumed she was asleep, and went to bed herself. Long after Cooper could hear her roommate's even breathing coming from across the room, she was still wide awake.

As she ran the events of the evening over and over in her mind, Cooper tried to decide what she could have said or done differently to make Ryan change his mind. Somehow this had to be her fault. Her parents had always taught her that every problem has a solution, she just had to find it. Well, she obviously hadn't looked hard enough for the answer this time and now there was no problem—or relationship—left to resolve.

Cooper never did get to sleep that night. Instead, she tortured herself with endless hours of introspection from which she was able to draw only one conclusion: *Here's one more thing I'm not good at.* And the reality of that observation haunted her.

C ooper didn't go to church that Sunday morning. It wasn't
that she was avoiding God, she just didn't want to spend
time with him in such a public place when she was feeling
so emotional. Instead, she drove around for a few hours, trying
to figure out how her life got so messed up. Mostly she just
sped back and forth on the freeway, allowing herself to get lost
again and again until about two that afternoon when she ended
up at Aunt Penny's.

"I wondered what happened to you this morning," her aunt
said after stepping aside to let Cooper in the door.

"I just wasn't up to it," Cooper explained.

By that time Penny had been able to get a good look at her
niece.

"That's obvious. What on earth happened to you?"

"Ryan and I broke up last night," Cooper told her.

Penny looked stunned. "Brian mentioned that he had talked
to you the other day and that you guys were having problems,
but he said you were pretty adamant about working them out."

"I did want to work them out. It was Ryan who did the
breaking up."

"Oh, Cooper, I'm so sorry," Penny cooed, pulling her into a hug.

Suddenly Cooper's exhaustion really hit her and she was certain that if Penny let go, she would crumple to the floor like a rag doll.

Penny ushered her into the living room, made some tea, and listened intently to the condensed version of the big break-up. Tears were streaming down Cooper's face by the time she was done and she had that "punched in the stomach" feeling all over again. It wasn't quite as shocking this time, but it was just as intense.

"I know you won't believe me if I tell you that you won't always feel this horrible, so I won't waste my breath. But if it helps any, in college I had a Ryan of my own, and I mean it when I say I know what you're going through."

"What do you mean, you had 'a Ryan' of your own?"

"Well his name wasn't Ryan, it was Joe. But other than that, the situations are pretty similar."

"And he dumped you?"

"He sure did, and I thought my life was over. I was so in love with him, I wanted to curl up and die when he left. I had been imagining what our life together would be like for so long that I didn't know how to imagine my life alone anymore."

"But why did he break up with you?" Cooper questioned.

"We just wanted really different things. I knew that, but I was convinced love would conquer all. He was a little more practical," Penny explained.

"So what happened to him? I mean where is he now, do you know?"

"He's a pastor in a small town in upstate New York. We still send each other Christmas cards every year. He met someone just a few months after we broke up and they got married a year later. They have three kids now."

"How did you get over him?" Cooper asked, eager for tips that would help her feel even the slightest bit better.

"There isn't any magic cure. It just took time, and even after I thought I was over him the feelings would come creeping back at odd moments."

"I don't know if all the time in the world could fix me right now."

"Oh, you'll be surprised. The heart is pretty good at bouncing back and I have to say that when I look at Joe's life now and where he's ended up, no matter how hard I try I can't imagine myself married to him. And if he hadn't seen that and broken up with me I would never have met Brian."

"But I don't want to meet anyone else," Cooper said between yawns.

"But you will some day. Look, you're really tired right now, why don't you lie down and take a nap?" Penny suggested. "Some sleep will make a difference, I promise."

Cooper didn't believe that anything would make the pain in her gut go away, but since she could barely keep her eyes open she curled up on the couch and covered up with a knitted blanket she'd found draped over the back of a chair. At least sleeping would allow a break from thinking about Ryan... unless he showed up in her dreams.

It was dark when she woke up, after eight, and the house was quiet.

"Penny?" she called out, sitting up on the couch and gathering the blanket around her shoulders.

"Right here, Cooper," she called from the kitchen. "I'm just having a late dinner. Do you want some soup? It's black bean."

"No thanks," Cooper responded without even trying to decide if she was hungry. "I think I should get back to campus, as much as I don't want to. I have to face it eventually."

"That's true," Penny agreed, "but you know if you need to get away this week you can always hang out here. It might be nice to have a safe place where there isn't the possibility of running into Ryan at every turn."

"Thanks, I'll keep that in mind."

"And remember, soon enough it will be spring break and that will give you some time away."

The blood drained from Cooper's face at her aunt's words and she dropped into the nearest chair with a dazed look on her face.

"What? What did I say?" Penny asked, her voice filled with concern.

"I'm supposed to go home with Ryan for spring break!" Cooper cried. "Now what am I going to do?"

"I completely forgot about that!" Penny said. "Well you know you're welcome to stay here, but I'm going with Brian to visit his parents in Arizona. It's time to do a little bonding with the future in-laws."

"I can't believe this didn't register before now," Cooper said. "He picked a great time to dump me, didn't he?"

"I know you're hurt, but I don't think Ryan did this just to ruin your spring break plans," Penny said. "He probably didn't even think about it."

"Well, I had better think about it," Cooper concluded, then muttered under her breath, "Oh, this is just great. Now I'm going to have to go home after all. It just gets better and better!"

"Look, why don't you try to forget about break right now. It's still two weeks away. You concentrate on getting through one day at a time," Penny charged, giving Cooper a big hug. "I know you can do it."

"I'm glad someone does."

"And call me this week if you need anything, even if it's just a shoulder to cry on," Penny called out to Cooper as she made her way down the front steps. Cooper waved without looking back and then got in her little red car and zoomed away into the night.

Aunt Penny had been right about one thing, getting some sleep had helped immensely. She still felt like she was wearing one of those lead aprons that dentists put on patients before taking x-rays, but now she had a little more energy to shoulder the extra weight. Just before she reached the PCU campus, she passed a sign that read St. Mark's Episcopal Church, but she couldn't remember why the name was familiar to her. Then it came to her. Sam had told her about an evening service there. Cooper glanced over as she drove, trying to catch a glimpse of the church. It was almost nine o'clock so Cooper was surprised to see people streaming into the traditional stone building. She was even more surprised when she turned her own car into the lot and parked.

What am I doing here? Cooper was still looking for an answer when she entered the lobby. Signs on the doors leading into the sanctuary warned that silence was expected throughout the service. *What kind of church service is this?*

Pushing the heavy door open, Cooper felt like she had entered another world. The church was dark except for a corner in the back where a group of men in white robes were singing in a musical style she couldn't classify. Not only were the wooden pews filled to capacity, but the cement floor was covered with students. Someone ushered Cooper to a side area where there was still a bit of room on the floor. She sat down on the cold concrete, never taking her eyes off the men singing. She was transfixed. For a few minutes anyway, Ryan and chemistry lab and parents and modeling agencies didn't exist, there was only that music. She wished she could stay there forever, just her and God and these men singing. All too soon it was over.

Cooper filed through the doors, noticing how those around her were careful to keep their vow of silence until they were all the way out of the church building, including a group of young boys with skateboards in front of her. She expected them to be joking and laughing, but they were surprisingly somber. Even after they were outside and had each lit up a cigarette, trying hard to look cool but not really succeeding, they were still quiet.

Walking through a light drizzle to her car, Cooper felt pounds lighter than she had when she entered the church. She had learned long ago that her faith wasn't just about feelings—in fact, sometimes it was more important to believe when she didn't feel anything at all—but every now and then, when things were especially hard and she was sure she couldn't go on, something would happen and she would feel God's love surround her as if he had reached down from Heaven and physically touched her. Then she could move forward, having been reminded that she wasn't alone.

10

G ee, I haven't seen you all day," Emily remarked. "Were you at your aunt's?"

"Yeah, I spent the afternoon there," Cooper informed her, careful not to offer any more information than was necessary. She still wasn't ready to tell Emily about the break-up.

"Well, I have a ton of studying to do, so I'll be out in the living room. Zoey's coming over, too," Emily explained, referring to her friend who lived down the hall. "Feel free to join us if you want."

"Thanks, but I'm really tired. I think I'll go to bed early."

"This will be two nights in a row that you're in bed before midnight! I should call the *Guinness Book of World Records*."

It was true, Cooper was always up late. Cooper offered up a quick prayer that Emily wouldn't get too suspicious about her change in sleeping patterns and start asking questions.

When she looked up again, Emily was carrying an armload of books into the other room. Cooper breathed a sigh of relief.

Soon, she heard Zoey's voice in the other room and Emily shushing her with her a "Quiet, Cooper's already asleep!" Then there was no sound at all.

When she woke up Monday morning Cooper felt great and hopped right out of bed, something she almost never did. But before she could even grab her robe and head for the shower, the memories came flooding back. Ryan was gone. She was a failure.

It was going to be a very long week.

She got ready for her first class, which ironically enough was Human Behavior, and was doing pretty well until she dug into her desk drawer for a pen. Inside, she found her anniversary present for Ryan, which started a trickle of tears. Cooper willed herself to stop, feeling angry at yet another emotional outburst, but the tears kept coming. It was several minutes before she was able to dry her eyes and repair the damage done to her make-up. She grabbed her backpack, stuffed the wrapped tickets inside, and rushed off to class. When she got there class had already started and she was late once again.

She tried really hard to focus on Professor Lichen's lecture, but she couldn't. Even on her best day she found him boring, and it made her uncomfortable the way he always brought the discussion around to sex. In her opinion, Professor Lichen was much more interested in the sex lives of his students than a professor should be, even in a class called Human Behavior.

Since she couldn't concentrate anyway, she decided to write Ryan a letter. Maybe it would be good to put her feelings down on paper. If she didn't like the way it turned out, she didn't have to send it.

With that decided, she flipped to a clean page in her notebook and began composing.

Dear Ryan,

I've had a little time to think since we talked on Saturday night and there were some things I didn't get a chance to say so I thought I'd write them down. I agree with you that there are some areas we need to work on, but I am very disappointed that you weren't willing to do just that. I can't believe that you were so quick to bail out. Is that what you plan on teaching your youth group when you're a pastor? To give up when things get hard? I'm sorry I didn't handle things too well the other night. It was immature of me to just walk away, but now that I have calmed down I would like to talk some more. I don't feel good about the way we left things the other day and I hope we can work it out. Please give me a call.

Cooper

P.S. I didn't get a chance to give these to you the other night. I hope you will still use them.

Cooper read over the note several times and when she couldn't think of anything to add, she carefully folded it and tucked it away in her backpack. She couldn't help feeling a sense of satisfaction as she zipped the note inside, as if she wasn't so powerless anymore. Of course, she would have to borrow someone's notes from class that day since she hadn't heard a single word of Professor Lichen's lecture, and there was sure to be a quiz the end of the week.

When class let out, Cooper hurried back to her dorm room to get an envelope, then rushed over to the campus post office. She put the tickets and note inside, licked the envelope, then turned it over and wrote "Ryan Stewart" in big letters across the front. She gave it a last look, popped it into the slot marked "on-campus mail," and went to check her own mailbox. She was pleasantly surprised to find a package slip inside.

As she waited in line to pick up the package, she tried to figure out who would be sending her something. Maybe it was from Claire and Alex; they had sent her several packages since she moved out west. Most contained silly things like rubber cockroaches and Empire State Building pencil sharpeners, just to make sure she didn't forget them. But the package wasn't from her high school friends; it was from her mother and was rather large.

She balanced the awkward box on her hip all the way back to her room then dumped it on the bed. It took several minutes of searching to locate a pair of scissors, but as soon as she found them she ripped the package open.

Cooper grabbed the note from her mother off the top while simultaneously peering inside the box. It was full of food—"snacks for your little road trip" her mother called them—and it contained all her favorites. There were dried cherries dipped in chocolate, white cheddar cheese popcorn, those little candy necklaces she and Claire were always wearing and munching on, and a special brand of crackers from Dean & Deluca, a gourmet grocery store downtown. Her mother had also included a gift for a Mr. and Mrs. Stewart. It was wrapped, so Emily couldn't tell what was inside, but she knew from the wrapping paper it was something from her mom's interior design shop. "Just a little show of appreciation for their hospitality," the note to Cooper read.

It was a very sweet gesture on her mom's part, especially since she really wanted Cooper to come home to New York for the school holiday. Cooper knew she should call and thank her mom, but she was hoping she and Ryan could work things out first; then she wouldn't need to explain to her mom why there wouldn't be a road trip, after all. She'd wait until after she heard from Ryan, then call her mom, she decided.

On her way to the cafeteria, Cooper ran into Emily and although she knew it was bound to happen eventually, she was still surprised when her roommate ran up to her and asked, "Are you all right?" her voice oozing sympathy.

"Sure, I'm okay."

"I heard about you and Ryan. Why didn't you tell me?"

"I don't know," Cooper answered honestly. "I guess I just wasn't ready to talk about it yet."

"I can't believe he did this to you, and right before our trip home! I guess you won't be coming now, will you?" Emily half asked, half stated.

"Not unless something changes between your brother and me in the next week or so."

"Oh," Emily responded glumly. "And I was really looking forward to showing you around at home. We would have had so much fun."

At the last statement tears began to blur Cooper's vision and she knew she was in danger of crying yet again. She didn't answer Emily, feeling afraid her voice would betray her emotions. The girls walked silently toward the cafeteria.

Cooper was pleasantly surprised to realize she was actually hungry after eating almost nothing the day before and skipping breakfast that morning as well. She loaded up her tray with a huge turkey sandwich, French fries, a green salad, the cafeteria's loose interpretation of chocolate mousse, and two glasses of Diet Coke. The girls then found an empty table on the perimeter of the dining room and proceeded to dig in.

Her sandwich was raised to her mouth and she was all ready to take a bite when she saw Ryan out of the corner of her eye. She hadn't noticed it when she sat down, but he was sitting just a few tables away, next to a pretty blond Cooper recognized from her calculus class. The girl was a cheerleader, Cooper remembered. Suddenly her appetite completely disappeared, and the sandwich began to slide from between her fingers. Cooper caught it in time and set it gently back on her plate. Then, pushing her tray away, she got up from the table.

"I need to get out of here," she numbly told Emily, stumbling past several chairs in her hurry to make it outside before the tears started.

I can't believe I sent him that note asking him to reconsider! He's obviously glad to be rid of me since he sure didn't wait very long to find someone else. And I gave him those Sonics tickets! How stupid could I be?

She was still beating herself up when she heard Ryan calling her name.

"Cooper, wait a minute."

Oh, great! Now to add to the humiliation, he's gonna see me crying! she thought as she swiped furiously at a few stray tears before turning around.

"Can I talk to you for a minute?" he asked. "I got your note and was going to call you when I got back to my dorm room."

"Oh, thanks a heap, but don't feel the need to cut your lunch short on account of me. You left your 'friend' in there all alone."

"Who, Debbie? We were just reviewing for a Spanish test together. And what does she have to do with us?"

"The last I knew there wasn't an 'us' anymore, so you can eat lunch with Debbie or anyone else," Cooper told him, trying to sound nonchalant. "It's really none of my business."

"Would you just stop it! I'm not looking for a new girlfriend!" Ryan insisted. "I've been miserable, too, and I really miss you. But I still think if we stayed together I'd only end up making you more miserable, and I like you too much to do that."

"You keep saying you like me too much to keep dating me, but that doesn't make any sense! If being apart is making us both miserable why don't we just get back together?" Cooper asked, sniffling between sentences.

"Because deep down we want different things. We *like* different things. If you really think about it, I know you'll agree with me."

Cooper finally accepted defeat. She was tired of arguing, and they weren't getting anywhere. Even if she didn't agree with him, it wasn't going to change his mind.

"I guess I'll see you around then," she said, turning to go.

"Cooper, wait."

She turned back around. She knew it was stupid but she couldn't help hoping he would say it was all a mistake. That he couldn't live without her. Instead he was holding out the tickets to the Sonics game.

"I can't keep these. It was really great of you to get them for me, but I can't take them the way things are between us. I'm sorry I ruined it for you."

But Cooper wouldn't take the tickets back.

"I can't get my money back for them and there's no way I'll use them. You might as well go. You know you want to," she urged.

Ryan seemed to consider it for a minute then quietly slid them back in his pocket.

"Just do me a favor," Cooper said. "Don't take Debbie."

Ryan smiled that smile that always made her feel like someone was squeezing her heart in his fist.

"Don't worry, there's no chance of that. I'll take one of the guys from the team."

Cooper nodded her approval.

"You know I really care about you, don't you?" Ryan asked.

Cooper grudgingly nodded again.

"Well that won't ever change. I'll always be here for you."

She couldn't think of anything to say in return.

"Can I give you a hug?" he asked before walking away, but Cooper shook her head.

"I don't think I can hug you right now," she told him honestly. She knew if she did she wouldn't ever let go.

11

With each passing day the dull ache in Cooper's chest felt a tiny bit better, but at the current rate of improvement she wouldn't feel even halfway human until well into the millennium. And she still wasn't eating. She had lost three pounds and her jeans, which were usually just a little loose, couldn't be worn without a belt now. She tried, but nothing looked good to her. She had even opened the chocolate cherries from her mom, but hadn't been able to choke down more than one or two.

Unable to put it off any longer, on Thursday night she called her mother and told her what had happened. Surprisingly, her mom was very sympathetic and sounded honestly upset that things hadn't worked out between Cooper and Ryan, even though she hadn't met him. Best of all, she didn't say anything trite like, "there are more fish in the sea" or "it obviously wasn't meant to be." She just listened, then offered to send Cooper a ticket home.

"I'll call you later and let you know where to pick it up," her mom said. "And sweetheart, it will be wonderful to see you, although I'm really sorry your other trip didn't work out."

And Cooper believed she was.

"See you next Friday, Mom."

An hour later Aunt Penny called.

"I just wanted to see how you were holding up this week. Are you doing any better?" Penny asked.

"A little," Cooper answered. "I feel like I'm being such a baby because I can't just snap out of this, but every time I begin to feel okay something reminds me of Ryan and it starts all over again."

"Well, I have the cure for that. How would you like to escape from PCU and all of your problems for a night?"

"I'd love to," Cooper said, with more enthusiasm than she'd felt in days. "What did you have in mind?"

"I thought getting off campus might be just what the doctor ordered so you and several of your closest friends are cordially invited to a slumber party at Chez Penny, Friday night, seven o'clock sharp, no boys allowed."

"That sounds great and the 'no boys' part certainly won't be a problem. But are you sure?"

"Of course. I'd love to have my favorite niece and her friends come trash my house. What's not to be sure of?"

"Well in that case, we'll be there. Everyone's cramming for midterms, but I'm sure we'll be ready to take a night off," Cooper said, adding, "What do you want us to bring?"

"Just yourselves. No, scratch that. Why don't you pick up some videos? Yeah, yourselves and some videos. I'll take care of the rest."

Just the thought of a party made Cooper smile. She hadn't had a slumber party in ages. Sometimes she and her suitemates would gather around the TV in the living room, eating PopTarts and watching Saturday morning cartoons while still in their pajamas, but that was as close as she had come recently.

Emily wasn't home, so she hurried next door to tell Kenzie the news. When she poked her head in her suitemate's room she wasn't surprised to see Allie there, too, her books and papers spread all over the other bed.

"I don't know *why* you don't just bring your clothes over and move in," Cooper said to Allie, causing Allie and Kenzie's heads to pop up in surprise.

"Because technically I already have a roommate," Kenzie explained, referring to Beth, their phantom suitemate who spent most of her waking hours at her boyfriend's in nearby Tacoma.

"That's what you'd like us to believe, but I don't think I've seen Beth more than twice this whole semester. I'm beginning to think it's all just a ploy so you can have a double room all to yourself. In fact, I bet you just hired that girl I *think* is Beth to pretend to be your assigned roommate. It's all a scam, but I'm onto you now, Dawson," Cooper charged, trying hard to keep a straight face.

"And you came in here to tell me this?" Kenzie asked.

"No, as a matter of fact I came in here to see who wants an excuse to blow off studying for midterms and eat tons of junk food this Friday night?"

"I do, I do!" Allie yelled, raising her hand and bouncing up and down on Beth's bed like a game show contestant.

"Well then Allie Raju, come on down! You've just won an all-expenses paid evening at…my Aunt Penny's!" Cooper announced in her best game show host voice.

"Gee, I was sort of hoping for Tahiti, but okay," Allie agreed.

"Now we'll need one more contestant," Cooper continued. "Is there a Kenzie Dawson in the audience? Why don't you join us here on stage?"

Kenzie made no move to get up.

When Cooper realized she wasn't going to be playing along she said "...or maybe not. How about if you join us for a slumber party Friday night instead? There will be videos, root beer, and your favorite suitemate: yours truly."

"I might be persuaded to take a little study break," Kenzie said, finally relenting.

"Great," Cooper said, happy to have something to look forward to at last. "It's a date!"

On Friday night, Cooper, Emily, Kenzie, Allie, and Zoey arrived at Penny's house in high spirits. Everyone was anxious to get off campus, even if it was for just one night, and any excuse to blow off studying for midterms was a welcome diversion.

"Hey, you made it," Penny said, giving Cooper a big hug.

"Yeah. For a while there it looked like we'd be spending the night at the video store, but we finally escaped," Cooper told her, dumping her stuff on the living room floor.

"Well, you're here now and that's what matters," Penny said. After the introductions were made, she added, "Girls, just drop your stuff anywhere and someone can put some music on if they want. It's a little too quiet in here for a party."

"Em, you're our resident DJ, why don't you be in charge of that?" Cooper directed, referring to the show her roommate did for PCU's campus radio station. "The CDs are right there. Penny's got all kinds of music. I'm sure you'll find some groups you like," she told her, pointing to a shelf next to Penny's stereo.

After making sure everything was under control in the living room, Cooper followed Penny into the kitchen and loudly deposited a box on the counter. As she began unpacking the popcorn and candy inside, Penny glanced over.

"What's that? I told you just to bring videos. You didn't have to get food, too."

"I didn't. It's compliments of Mom," Cooper explained, telling her aunt about the care package for the trip that wasn't going to happen.

"In that case, we'll put it to good use!"

"That's what I was counting on," Cooper told her.

"Oh, look, candy necklaces!" Allie announced, peeking into Cooper's box.

Cooper pulled out a handful of them and said, "Go to town."

"Not so fast," Allie said, slipping a necklace on Cooper before heading back into the living room to distribute the rest of the edible jewelry.

Cooper had returned to unpacking the food when Penny said, "You look like you could stand to eat all that junk food yourself. You're skin and bones."

"I know, I know," Cooper said, hanging her head. "I'm trying to eat, but I just haven't been hungry."

"Well, we'll fix that," Aunt Penny said. With that she began pulling platters and dishes out of the refrigerator and uncovering the bowls that lined the counter. In a matter of minutes the kitchen table was covered with enough food to feed an entire football team.

"Do you think I overdid it?" she asked, surveying the huge quantities of snacks she had put out.

"Maybe just a smidge," Cooper said gently.

"Well, it's not like I have slumber parties every day, you know."

"Oh, no!" Cooper consoled. "I'm sure everything will be gone by morning. It looks great." As if on cue, her stomach rumbled loudly.

"See, I told you!" she laughed.

After sampling the spinach dip and a mini quiche, Cooper called to the girls in the other room: "Soup's on!" and they all came scrambling in.

As they stood around the table filling up plates and popping open cans of soda, Penny chimed in, "Now, girls, if you want something a little more substantial we can always order pizza."

Everyone just looked at the table and laughed.

"No, I think this will last us until fall," Kenzie pointed out. "But thanks."

"Well, you never know. You might get hungry again later. Just keep it in mind."

"We'll be sure and do that," Emily said, popping a dip-laden chip into her mouth. Even Cooper was eating.

With full plates, everyone made their way into the living room, and blankets and pillows were spread across the floor as they prepared for the first movie. It was a romantic comedy and while it was an interesting story, Cooper couldn't stop her mind from wandering. She wondered if Ryan had gone to the basketball game that night and who he went with. She wondered if he was thinking of her at all. Finally, she wondered if she would ever stop wondering…if she would ever not look for him in the cafeteria or in the Student Union Building or The Snack Shop.

The second movie was more of the same and afterward, talk of the romantic storyline led to talk of relationships in general. Soon the girls were each telling the story of her first crush, her first date, her first kiss.

With the change of topic, Cooper noticed Emily eyeing her with concern. But silly stories about boys from high school didn't bother her. In fact, most of the stories were so hilarious she found herself really laughing for the first time in days. Cooper even joined in the storytelling, admitting that when she was in the fifth grade she and her friend Claire had a contest to see who could kiss the most boys in their class.

"Claire won with only three kisses," she explained, "but I found out later she had paid each of the boys a quarter so she was disqualified. Still, I couldn't help being impressed since I knew that even with the promise of cold hard cash I couldn't have bribed anyone to kiss me that year. Of course, I like to think it had something to do with the fact that I was almost a foot taller than most of the boys in my class."

"Oh, I'm sure that was it," Emily teased.

"Then in junior high we moved on to making lists of what our ideal boyfriend would be like," Cooper told the group. "I found one last year when I was packing for college and I couldn't believe how shallow I was at twelve."

"Everyone was shallow at twelve," Kenzie pointed out.

"No, I'm talking really, *really* shallow. The most important thing was that he had enough money to buy me gum from the school store every day."

"Have you made any lists recently?" Zoey asked.

"Not in the last six months," Cooper said, a thought of Ryan flickering through her mind, "but Claire and I have sort of an informal list going that we add to every now and then."

"What's on it?" Zoey asked, leaning forward with interest.

"Actually, they're more like rules. We made a pact that we won't date anyone who weighs less than us, wears more earrings than we do, has longer hair…that's all I can think of right now. Oh, or anyone with hair on his back. That is definitely out."

"Eeeeeeuw!" Emily squealed. "That is completely disgusting."

"Well, haven't you ever been at the beach and you see some older guy whose back is so hairy he looks like he's wearing a sweater?" Cooper asked.

"It's good to see your standards aren't based on anything shallow now that you're older," Allie joked.

"Hey, you guys asked. Obviously other things are important, too. They're just not as much fun to talk about."

"Let's talk about 'em anyway," Emily proposed. "What would your ideal guy be like?"

"He'd be breathing," Zoey said. "That's about the extent of my list."

Everyone laughed, but Emily persisted.

"No, really. I'm serious, you guys."

"Then you go first," Cooper told her, putting her roommate on the spot.

"That's fine with me. I've had plenty of dateless nights to think about it."

Emily then proceeded to describe a guy who sounded suspiciously like Dan, a coincidence that wasn't lost on her audience.

"Okay, let me take a stab at it now," Cooper said. "I want someone tall with brown hair, laid back, casual, involved in his church, close to his family, not from the city, *any* big city," she described.

"No offense, but that's not the kind of guy I picture you with," Kenzie said. "You're gonna be with some artsy, sophisticated, big city guy. Probably from New York."

"But that's not what I want at all!" Cooper protested.

"Why not? I know you're still pretty bummed about you and Ryan, but...okay, true confession: I never really thought you two were a match made in heaven. You guys are *so* different," Kenzie continued.

"Maybe I'm tired of being different. Maybe I want to be more like Emily," Cooper explained. "You know, laid back, casual, *normal*."

"You want to be like me?" Emily sputtered. "I would give anything to have *your* life! Well, except for the dating my brother part, but the rest of it, definitely!"

Cooper just shrugged. "You don't know how lucky you are. You have a normal family, your parents don't have any expectations of you except that you be happy, you have brothers and sisters. Your life is just so normal."

"And it would bore you to death," Emily told her roommate. "Why can't we ever want to be who we already are?"

"I think every eighteen-year-old girl asks that question," Penny said from her perch on the couch.

"Is there an answer?" Emily asked.

"No. But if you're lucky, you learn to like who you are enough that you eventually stop asking the question."

"Have you stopped?" Cooper probed.

"For the most part," Penny answered, nodding her head. "Most days I'm pretty happy with exactly who God made me to be, although it's my expert opinion that no woman is ever really happy with her thighs."

The conversations went on like this for hours and it wasn't until sometime after three that the talking finally stopped altogether and everyone was asleep. They never did get around to watching the third movie, but judging by the size of the mess they had made, the slumber party was a huge success.

12

The best thing about exam week was that it afforded Cooper little time to think about Ryan. It passed more quickly than she would have imagined, however. Now that it was over, she couldn't believe she had made it through another week of midterms and that she would soon be back in New York. Claire and Alex had been excited when she told them she was coming, but she was still apprehensive.

The flight was uneventful and the man sitting next to Cooper slept the entire time so she watched the movie, ate her chewy airline chicken dinner, and had listened to three of the eight CDs she'd packed when they touched down. It was almost midnight when Cooper made her way down to the baggage claim at La Guardia Airport.

"Hey, Miss, need a ride into the city?" a voice behind her asked. Cooper turned to decline the offer, assuming it was one of the gypsy cabs—the drivers without their taxi licenses who couldn't be relied on to take passengers where they wanted to go and were even known to rob some of their "fares"—but it was Alex, and peeking over his shoulder was Claire.

Her friends looked just like she remembered. Claire's chestnut brown hair was still long, hanging more than halfway down her back, and she was wearing a black vinyl skirt, black boots, and a tangerine colored T-shirt with some Japanese cartoon character on the front. Alex was in his usual khakis topped with a plain black T. The only difference Cooper saw was Alex's hair seemed a little shorter, and he now had a goatee.

"What are you guys doing here?" Cooper screamed with delight.

"Picking up our long-lost friend, of course," Claire explained.

"But cab fare out here is almost twenty dollars! Why didn't you just wait at the apartment for me?"

"We *were* waiting at the apartment, but your mom thought it would be nice if we picked you up so she slipped us a twenty, and we were gone," Alex said.

"I think it had more to do with getting rid of us than her thinking you had forgotten how to hail a cab. Alex spent almost an hour critiquing your parents' video collection and your mom made her offer right after that," Claire confided conspiratorially.

"Excuse me?" Alex said, doing his best to sound offended. "I was simply helping your parents out by sharing my vast film knowledge with them."

The girls rolled their eyes at each other. Cooper hated to admit it, even to herself, but it felt kind of good to be back. And as the cab they were riding in came up out of the midtown tunnel and turned to head up Third Avenue, all the twinkling lights and honking horns—even the car alarms—seemed to be welcoming her home.

Her parents were waiting up when Cooper and her friends arrived at the apartment, but soon after they'd said their hellos, they were off to bed. Cooper's mother had to meet with some clients bright and early, and her dad was usually in the office before seven, so he'd had a long day, too. Cooper was still wide awake since it was before ten back in Seattle, and Claire and Alex were used to staying up late.

"So what do you want to do first?" Alex asked.

"I really don't know," Cooper answered honestly, absently petting Winston Churchill, her bulldog that was named after Britain's jowly former prime minister. "What do we want to do first, Winston?" she asked, looking expectantly at her dog. But he just drooled and snorted happily. Cooper had been so upset about the break-up with Ryan, and so immersed in studying for midterms, that she hadn't given her vacation plans any thought. She hadn't even really let it sink in that she would be in New York the whole week, let alone consider how she might fill all that Ryan-free time. Fortunately, her friends had taken matters in hand.

"It's a good thing you have us around then," Claire added, "because we took the liberty of working up a little schedule for you."

Cooper was confused. "A schedule?"

Alex pulled a folded sheet of paper out of his jacket pocket and held it out to her. It was a schedule all right, done on the computer, and under each day was a list of activities they had planned for her. Neither of their spring breaks coincided with Cooper's, so they would both be attending classes during the week, but they had worked around that. Cooper looked at the top items on the list, which told her that she was spending her first full day back in Central Park with Claire and Alex, then having dinner with her parents.

"We didn't want to hog you the whole day so we told your mom she could have you after six tomorrow."

98

"That was very generous of you," Cooper said.

On Sunday she was scheduled to attend an Easter concert at the Brooklyn Tabernacle with Claire and Alex, then they were all coming back to her parents' for a big Easter brunch with Claire's parents, as well. That wasn't too surprising. Cooper's and Claire's parents co-owned the interior design business where they both worked and had been close friends for years.

"Your mom invited Alex last week before the video incident. He might be uninvited now," Claire teased.

"Mrs. Ellis loves me like her own son," Alex said confidently. "Of course I'm still invited."

"That's debatable, but let's get back to this schedule," Cooper said.

On Monday morning she was shopping for fabric with Claire in the garment district while Alex was in class, then they were all meeting up for dinner at the little coffee shop near her parent's that night.

"I have a project due on Friday, a dress I've been designing, and it's so much easier to make it for someone else so I thought you could be my guinea pig." Claire proposed. "It's a great deal since you get a new dress out of it."

During high school Cooper had spent hundreds of hours as Claire's own personal mannequin. She complained a lot during the actual fittings and had been poked more times than she could remember, but she had to admit the clothes Claire made for her were exquisite.

"Count me in," Cooper said, then reading ahead she noticed that on Wednesday she was scheduled for a fitting with Claire. "Obviously you already did," she added wryly.

"I knew you'd say yes," Claire explained, grinning a little sheepishly.

Tuesday included shopping in SoHo and the East Village in

the afternoon, since both of her friends had classes that morning. On Wednesday, Claire needed her for a fitting of the dress, Thursday was blocked out as a free day, and on Friday Cooper and Alex had a date with the Museum of Radio and Television in Midtown.

"You'll love it there," Alex told her. "We pick out old radio or TV shows we want to watch then go to a viewing booth where they're all set up. Right now, I'm doing a study of film stars who started out in television, so I need to check out some old shows. There's one called "The Courtship of Eddie's Father," which has one episode with a really young Jodie Foster playing a bully," Alex added with enthusiasm.

Cooper looked back at her list. Following that little trip into TV past, she and Alex would be meeting Claire at school, after she picked up her grade for the dress she was making for Cooper. Next they were going out for a movie and then to a little coffeehouse near the theater. Saturday was her big farewell video night, and she flew out on Sunday.

"At least I won't be bored," Cooper mused.

"We'll make sure of that. By the end of the week you'll wonder how you've lived without us for so many months," Alex said.

"You'll probably be having such a good time you won't even want to go back to Seattle. You'll just send for your things and transfer to a local school," Claire added.

"Don't push your luck. I really like PCU, and you don't know what you're missing by not living on campus," Cooper told them.

"At least we have you for the week. We'll just have to make the most of it," Claire said.

"Seriously though, you guys, it's really good to see you! If I could pack you both in my suitcase and take you back to Seattle with me, I'd do it in a minute," Cooper said, then added, "even if I had to pay extra because my bags weighed so much."

"Oh, no, you don't!" Alex responded. "You may want to go and play nature girl in the Wild West, but I'm staying put. Seattle will just have to live without me."

"And if Alex isn't going, I can't go," said Claire, snuggling closer to her new boyfriend and kissing his stubbly cheek.

"Oh, please! You guys are making me sick."

"At least we spared you the pain of fixing you up with one of Alex's eligible roommates," Claire said. "They saw a picture of the three of us on Alex's desk and now they want to meet you."

"Oh, great!" Cooper groaned.

"Hey, Justin's not that bad," Alex countered. "He's the one I share a room with. I could just invite him along to the movie on Friday, no pressure," he suggested.

"No way," Claire said, shooting down the idea even before Cooper had a chance to. "I've been in that apartment," she explained to her friend, "and his roommates are pigs. Justin is better than Corey, but there's no way I'd subject you to either of them."

"Well, thank you," Cooper responded, feeling relieved. "And just because you guys are so annoyingly happy doesn't mean everyone needs to be paired up, you know? This isn't the Ark, so if it's all the same to you both I think I'd like to just fly solo for a while."

"We understand," Claire answered for both of them, nodding solemnly. Cooper had talked on the phone to her for almost two hours the week after she and Ryan broke up, so Claire understood what she was going through perhaps better than anyone.

"But if you change your mind, Justin is ready and waiting," Alex teased, not quite so sensitive to Cooper's need for a little time to heal.

After raiding the refrigerator and making plans for the girls to meet Alex at the park the next day, the friends said goodnight. Cooper followed them to the elevator, which would take Claire to the downstairs apartment she still shared with her parents. Alex waved good-bye, too, on his way out to catch the subway downtown.

"See you in the morning," Cooper called just before the elevator doors slid closed. As she closed her own door, making sure Winston Churchill had followed her back inside, Cooper realized that even though it was still relatively early in Seattle she was exhausted. Midterm week, the long flight, and the excitement of seeing her old friends again were finally taking their toll.

She headed down the hall to her old room and got ready for bed. Pulling out a T-shirt and pair of flannel boxers, her pajamas of choice, Cooper couldn't help thinking how wrong it was that she was home. Despite the comfort she felt at seeing her old friends, it still seemed like she should be at Ryan and Emily's right now, meeting the rest of the Stewarts, resting up after the long drive, looking at baby pictures of her boyfriend and seeing where he had come from. Instead, she was in her old room that her mother had decorated with everything perfectly coordinated, nothing out of place.

Under the covers with the light out and her dog snoring, Cooper tried to remember the last night she had spent in that room. At the time, she had looked forward to leaving New York behind and starting a new life in Seattle. For a while she thought she had found that new life with Ryan, but now she wondered. Maybe Claire and Alex were right. Maybe by the end of the week she would be ready to stay in New York.

Holding tight to Winston's leash, the girls headed over to the park. As they walked, Cooper filled Claire in on exam week and other bits of news while Claire told her all about design school. She was still describing the dress she was going to make for Cooper when they entered the park. Passing through Strawberry Fields, the memorial to John Lennon who was shot in front of his apartment building just across the street, the girls darted in front of several rollerbladers in an attempt to get to the other side of the path. Crossing from the west side of the park to the east, Cooper was flooded with memories of afternoons spent there.

When she was little, her parents had brought her to the park almost every weekend to visit the Alice in Wonderland statue, wander through the zoo, and ride the carousel. Later, Cooper, Alex, and Claire had come to skate or to lie in the sun and read or listen to the radio. She couldn't imagine her childhood without that park.

"Look, there's Alex," Claire pointed out. He was wearing loose khakis and a faded green T-shirt with one of his thrift-store-find shirts over the top and a pair of black suede tennis shoes. His short brown hair was glinting in the sun as he carried on a conversation with an old man on the edge of the boat pond.

He noticed Cooper and Claire and smiled, but continued to talk. When he finally joined them, nearly twenty minutes had elapsed.

"Why the sudden interest in boats?" Cooper asked.

"Yeah, are you planning to quit film school and start hanging here at the boat pond with the other eccentrics?" Claire chimed in.

"I just liked talking to him," Alex shrugged. "He's an interesting guy. You never know, maybe I could use him as a subject for one of the short films I have to do this year."

"That would be cool. He seemed kind of lonely," Cooper said.

"I think he is. He told me his wife died a few years back and his son lives in Baltimore, so he's all by himself. He said he hangs out here almost every day."

"You'll definitely have to come back and visit him again then," Claire told him. "We can come together."

"It's a date, but now I'm all yours for the rest of the day, so...hot dog, anyone?"

The trio headed over to a hot dog cart on a little side path and placed their orders.

"I bet they don't have anything like this in Seattle," Alex remarked as they watched the steaming hot dogs being placed in the buns.

"I have to admit they don't," Cooper answered. "And you know, it's funny, I never even missed them. But now that I'm here that smell brings it all back and I can't believe I've lasted for so many months without a real New York hot dog."

They slathered on mustard and relish, then walked as they ate. There was music coming from somewhere just north of the zoo, so they decided to check it out. They strolled along, eating their lunch, remembering to drop pieces for Winston, until they reached the spot where the concert was taking place. A group was playing some sort of Caribbean music and the friends sat on a patch of grass to listen for a while.

Sitting there soaking up the sun and the music, Cooper remembered the night she and Ryan had planned the Mt. Rainier hike, and the argument they'd had about her never going outside. When she was in New York she went outside all the time, walking everywhere. It was just in Seattle where nothing was within walking distance and she had to drive to get anywhere that Cooper was always indoors. She wondered if Ryan was outside enjoying the sunshine, too.

Cooper sighed. It was an unusually beautiful spring day, not muggy and humid, but not too windy either, and as she and her friends reminisced about old times, Ryan began to seem further and further away. Only when she saw Alex put his arm lazily around Claire's shoulder did Cooper feel a little twinge of sadness.

That night, however, during dinner with her parents, Ryan had more time to creep into Cooper's thoughts. Usually she loved the restaurant, but this time she was distracted by all the cozy-looking couples at The Grand Ticino.

"Honey, did you hear me? I asked when you're going to stop by the modeling agency," Mrs. Ellis asked, straightening the jacket of her red linen suit.

"What?" Cooper asked by way of reply, absently twirling her fettucine around on her fork.

"I said when are you going by Yacomina? Didn't you promise Tara you'd stop in if you were in town?"

Leave it to her mom to remember something like that. When Cooper didn't answer her mother persisted.

"You could go first thing Monday morning and get it out of the way so you can enjoy the rest of the week with your friends," she proposed.

"I can't," Cooper was able to answer honestly. "I'm going fabric shopping with Claire on Monday. She has a big project due the end of the week—a dress—and she's fitting it on me. Then we're meeting up with Alex."

"Maybe Tuesday then," Mrs. Ellis said, not giving up.

Cooper tried to remember what was on the schedule for

that day, but unfortunately she couldn't. Anyway, she had a feeling that was a day both Claire and Alex were in class.

"I guess I could stop by Tuesday," Cooper finally agreed while her mother smiled approvingly.

It was the least she could do, go see Tara and tell her face-to-face that she wasn't going to Italy that summer and wasn't planning on working for Bella in Seattle, either. There had to be a more meaningful way to spend her summer and her free time at school. Yes, Cooper thought with determination, her short-lived modeling career was over once and for all.

13

On Easter morning, Cooper, Claire, and Alex got up early and took the subway out to the Park Slope area where the Brooklyn Tabernacle was located. It wasn't the church they normally attended—the three usually went to the afternoon service at a church on the Upper West Side—but it was a tradition among them to go to the Easter service at Brooklyn Tab. Claire's and Cooper's parents had always gone to a more conservative church in Midtown, but there wasn't really anything for Claire and Cooper there, so the girls had switched over a few years back with their parents' blessing.

In the last year or two, though, Cooper's parents had stopped going to church altogether. At first Cooper alternated between trying to force them to go back and ignoring the whole subject, but neither technique worked very well. This Easter, she had worked up the courage to broach the subject the night before with her mom, but Mrs. Ellis said she had too much to do to prepare for brunch.

"I don't know what to do," Cooper confided to her friends as the #4 train careened through New York City's dark underground tunnels toward Flatbush Avenue. "My parents used to

be such strong Christians when I was little, but now...."
Cooper let her words trail off. She wasn't sure what had
changed.

"Have you ever just come right out and asked them?" Alex
asked.

"Not really," Cooper admitted. "I think I'm afraid of what I'd
hear."

"Maybe I could ask my parents," Claire suggested.

"It just seems that as the parents they should be the ones
trying to find a way to get *me* to go church. Why does everything in my life always seem so backward?"

Cooper's friends just shrugged in response. They had all
been going to church together for years, so it was easy for them
to discuss spiritual things, to wrestle with and argue over certain passages or issues. But when it came to their parents, they
were at a loss. Alex's parents had never gone to church; he had
started coming with the girls back in junior high. Claire's parents had always been regular attenders, but were never really
involved beyond that. Cooper's parents were the ones who
seemed really committed; then it all just stopped.

Sitting in one of the long, dark wood pews that morning in
Brooklyn, Cooper offered up a prayer for her parents, asking
God to somehow let them find their way back to Him. *Just show
me what to do, God, and I'll do it. Anything,* she whispered. She
also prayed for Penny and Brian in Arizona and for her PCU
friends, even Ryan. She couldn't help praying that maybe he'd
be praying for her at church that morning in Oregon. She knew
it wasn't really right, it wasn't an unselfish prayer, but she was
still struggling with letting go. Finally, she put Ryan and her
parents out of her mind and tried to focus on the Easter service.

Every year it hit her again that she would never be able to
fully comprehend what Jesus had done for her...that someone

so perfect had been willing to die for all the stupid mistakes Cooper Ellis had made and would still make in her life. She was still considering this as they made their way back to the subway station.

"I'm starving," Alex announced, breaking into her thoughts.

"It's nice to see that the service was able to raise you to such a spiritual level," Cooper told him.

"Hey, I can be spiritual and still be hungry," Alex pointed out.

"I know, I'm sorry," Cooper said. "I guess I'm just being a little hyper-sensitive. Easter always brings home how much God has really done for me, which only seems to emphasize how little I do for him in return."

"I don't think that's how God sees it," Claire told her friend, "But if that's how you feel, why don't you find a way to do more?"

"That's just it!" Cooper wailed as their train pulled up to the platform. Seating herself on one of the hard plastic benches facing her friends, she took a deep breath and continued: "You both know what you want to do and have some talent God has given you that you can use to make a difference. Alex has his films and you have your designing—I can't think of two industries that need Christ more—but what do I have?"

"Just because you haven't found something you love yet, doesn't mean you can't make a difference," Claire pointed out. "There are plenty of things you can do."

"Like what?"

"Uh…I…I don't know," Claire answered honestly. "I'm sure if you look around, though, you'll just fall into something. Like last year when I was helping to organize the fashion show at school and we were trying to find some way to make it different. Well, there was a story on the news that night about all the homeless people who were expected to literally freeze to death that winter. So it hit me: let's make the admission price be a scarf, gloves, or a used coat that we could give to the homeless. Then someone else came up with the idea to auction off the designs and give that money to the shelter down the street from school."

"But I'm not organizing any fashion shows in the near future," Cooper said.

"I was simply making a point," Claire said. "You know what I mean."

"I know, it just seems like you guys are always falling into these things and I'm still struggling to figure out where to go and what to do with my life."

"Maybe God just wants to know you'll follow Him even if you don't know where he's leading you," Alex proposed.

"And I will," Cooper said. "It would just be so much easier, though, if he'd give me a little glimpse of what's ahead."

"Wouldn't we all like that!" Claire laughed, standing in front of the subway car's door as it pulled into the station.

Cooper followed Claire and Alex up the stairs that led out of the station and to her parent's apartment.

"It smells wonderful in here," Alex enthused, heading straight for the kitchen and popping a few grapes in his mouth.

"Everything is all ready. We were just waiting for you kids," Mrs. Ellis explained.

In a matter of minutes the table was filled with strawberry crepes, a seafood quiche, a huge fresh fruit salad, a basket full of warm, buttery croissants, and a crystal pitcher of fresh-squeezed orange juice. Thirty minutes later, everyone was leaning back in their chairs, their stomachs full.

Cooper, Claire, and Alex volunteered to do the dishes while the two older couples went out for a walk, "to let their food digest."

"Do you really think walking helps your food digest?" Alex asked when they were gone.

"I have absolutely no idea," Cooper told him. "Why do you care?"

"I was just wondering," he answered. "I mean, it sounds reasonable, like it would have an easier time of things than if you were, say lying down because then it's fighting gravity, but I just wondered."

"You are so weird," Cooper said, tossing him a dishtowel so he could dry.

"But I like you anyway," Claire told him, giving him a hug.

"Okay, that's enough of that," Cooper declared, aiming the sprayer from the kitchen sink at them. "Back to work, or I shoot."

Her friends knew her well enough to know she'd use it, too. Claire quickly went to finish clearing the table, putting the few leftovers that remained in plastic containers or covering them with foil. Cooper passed the clean dishes one by one to Alex who dried them and put them away. Her friends probably knew where things went in her parents' kitchen as well as she did, Cooper figured. They had spent enough time there. When the kitchen was all clean, they hung out and watched boring Sunday afternoon TV for the rest of the day.

"Don't forget, we're going fabric shopping early tomorrow," Claire reminded her before she left later that afternoon. Alex had already left earlier as he had some studying to do before class the next day.

"I won't, I won't," Cooper said.

"Pick me up at nine o'clock then, okay?"

"Got it. Nine o'clock," Cooper said confidently to her friend, but as she started to close the door she mumbled "some vacation," under her breath. She didn't get up that early when school was in session.

111

"I heard that," Claire called from the hallway where she stood waiting for the elevator.

"Heard what?" Cooper innocently asked. "I said 'some dedication,'" she inaccurately pointed out.

"That's not what I heard," Claire said, "but I'll still see you at nine sharp."

"Yeah, yeah, whatever you say."

Cooper was still trying to wake up as she stood in Claire's bedroom doorway the next morning.

"So here's the design," Claire said, holding a sketch of the dress out to Cooper. Her eyes were mere slits, but Cooper managed to take it in and comment halfway intelligently.

"I like what you did with the low waist. It's very 20s," Cooper observed.

"That's exactly the look I was going for!" Claire exclaimed happily. "I knew you would understand what I was trying to do. It's so great having you home."

Claire gave Cooper a little hug and they were out the door.

"You know, I'd be even more supportive and encouraging after lunch. It's not too late to get a few more hour's sleep," Cooper proposed as the elevator carried them down to the lobby.

"We'll stop on the corner and I'll buy you a coffee."

"Make it a cappuccino and you've got yourself a mannequin."

"Cappuccino it is then," Claire said, linking her arm through Cooper's and dragging her friend down the street. "You drive a hard bargain."

"I think you're getting off pretty easy myself," Cooper replied.

Cooper was still trying to wake up, gulping her large cappuccino, as they stepped onto the subway train that would take them downtown. When they got off at 57th Street she felt a little better, and once they entered the first fabric store Claire's enthusiasm began rubbing off on her.

The first stop was a cavernous shop with bolts of fabric leaning against walls and stacked haphazardly on makeshift tables. The fashion district was full of similar discount shops, lined up one after another, that were really nothing more than converted warehouses. But people didn't shop there for the decor; they came because the prices were the lowest in town, and even the most obscure fabrics could be found with a little patience.

"What do you think of this?" Claire asked mischievously while showing Cooper a length of stretchy leopard print.

"Over my dead body," Cooper responded.

"I was just teasing. Spandex isn't really my fabric of choice," Claire explained. "But I was hoping for something different. I don't want to choose something too obviously 20s."

"It's not obviously 20s, but it certainly is obvious," Cooper pointed out disdainfully.

"What about this?" Claire asked, moving on to a bolt of dark green fabric.

Cooper ran a piece of the fabric between her fingers. "It's nice," she offered.

"But it's just not right," Claire finished for her, setting the bolt back on the shelf.

"Yeah, I like it but not for this dress."

They went through five other shops with the same result. Finally, in a crowded little store with bolts of fabric piled to the ceiling they found what they were looking for: a beautiful piece of washed silk in a deep shade of purple. It was heavy, but not too heavy, and unlike regular silk it wasn't shiny but had a matte finish. In fact, the texture and color were like nothing either girl had seen before.

"This will hang just perfectly," Claire announced to her friend.

At the register it was measured and there was just enough fabric with a sixteenth of a yard to spare. Both girls breathed a sigh of relief and the clerk even threw in the extra amount as a bonus.

"You never know when you might need a little extra," he pointed out, winking at the girls.

"I can't wait to get home and start cutting this out," Claire said as they left the store.

"Can we get something to eat first?" Cooper asked.

"I'll make you a salad at home. You can eat and I'll cut."

"Okay, okay, but you know you're a slave driver. You're going to be one of those designers they expose in the tabloids for running a sweatshop," Cooper told her very focused friend.

"That's not even funny. That's a big problem in the fashion business," Claire explained.

"I know. I'm witnessing it firsthand. I've been on my feet for four hours with no break. I'm going to call the union on you," Cooper threatened.

"You don't belong to a union," Claire pointed out wryly. "And besides, I said I'd feed you and I'm making you a dress, aren't I? How many bosses provide their employees with free food and clothing?"

"I guess all the ones who don't pay their employees," Cooper joked.

"Well one day when I have my own line of stores you can model in my shows and I'll pay you exorbitant amounts of money, okay?"

"Oh, I'm sure you'll want some big name by then. Besides, I've pretty much quit modeling, and I've never done runway work."

"You wouldn't even make an exception and come out of retirement for me?" Claire asked, trying to sound offended.

"Okay. If you ever have your own show in Bryant Park I'll work the runway for you. You have my word on it."

"That's better, now let's get home. I'm getting a little hungry myself."

14

On Tuesday morning, Cooper woke with a feeling of dread. She was going to the Yacomina office that morning to meet with Tara. She knew she needed to get it over with, but at the same time she couldn't help wishing she could put it off awhile longer. At dinner the night before, Claire and Alex had encouraged her to just be honest with Tara. If she didn't really want to model anymore then why waste Tara's time?

Walking across town to Yacomina Models gave Cooper a little extra time to think. Moving along Lexington Avenue, surrounded by the usual midweek crowds, Cooper tried to imagine what she would say, but she didn't know how to explain all of her jumbled thoughts to Tara. All too soon she reached the building where Yacomina had its offices on the third floor. Riding up in the elevator she had taken so many times before, Cooper whispered a quick prayer, asking God to make it clear to her what she was supposed to do once and for all.

Tara was on the phone when Cooper entered the office so she took a seat in the lobby area. As she began thumbing through a magazine, a tall, familiar-looking brunette about

Cooper's age took a seat next to her.

"Didn't we work on a shoot together last summer?" the girl said just as Cooper began reading an article entitled "How to Win Your Man Back."

Cooper tore her eyes away from the magazine for a minute.

"They shot it at the beach?" the girl prompted, but Cooper still stared blankly.

"In any case, I'm Jacinta," the girl said, holding out a hand.

"And I'm Cooper. I'm sorry I'm drawing a blank on working together, but you do look familiar to me."

"Yeah, I'm told I have that kind of face," Jacinta explained with a shrug. "It's worked for me so far, though, so I'm not complaining."

"I can see why," Cooper told her. A lot of models didn't look like anything special when they weren't made up, with the only clue to their profession often being their height. But Jacinta was striking, even with no make-up and her golden-brown hair pulled back in a ponytail.

"It's weird since we're with the same agency that I haven't run into you more often, though," Jacinta said with a thoughtful look. "I'm in and out of this office a couple times a week at least."

"I've been in Seattle going to school," Cooper explained.

"Really? What school?" Jacinta asked, excitement creeping into her voice.

"Pacific Cascades University, why?" Cooper replied.

"Have you ever heard of Seattle Pacific University?"

"Of course," Cooper answered. SPU was a Christian College in northern Seattle that was about the same size as PCU. "I even considered applying there. Do you know someone who goes there?"

"Yes, well, sort of," Jacinta told Cooper a bit cryptically

before explaining further. "I mean, I'm going there. I was just accepted to start in the fall. I'll be a twenty-year-old freshman, but I've been saving for the last two years, and if I get some good jobs in the next six months I should be able to pay for school all on my own, which is a good thing because my parents refuse to help. They think I'm becoming a religious freak."

"There are worse things to be. But hey, congratulations on getting accepted!"

"Thanks, I can barely wait," Jacinta replied. "So what's the work like in Seattle? Do you get sent out on many jobs?"

"Oh, I'm not with an agency there," Cooper admitted. "I haven't been doing any modeling since I left New York."

"Then what are you doing here?" Jacinta asked.

"Well, sort of quitting, I guess."

"But why? Is it too hard to work and go to school?"

"No," Cooper answered honestly. "I haven't really even tried it. I'm just tired of the business, all the dishonest people and the egos. You know, you're the first Christian I've met since I started out?"

"Maybe that's a reason to keep doing it, right there. I wouldn't be a Christian at all if another model hadn't invited me to a Bible study in Germany when I was working there. I was a total mess, but God really turned my life around and now when I run into other models and photographers I used to work with they see this huge difference in me. It's so cool to be able to tell them who changed my life. It's like my own personal little mission field."

Cooper just stared at her coworker. She had never thought of modeling as a ministry opportunity before. "I don't know if I could be that bold," Cooper said.

"I couldn't by myself, either. But I have a lot of support and that makes all the difference in the world," Jacinta explained.

"There's this group that meets every week in the theater district and they're all involved in the industry—bookers, photographers and models, even make-up artists—and they're great. They have a Bible study and a chance to bring up any issues or work-related problems and get input from others who've been there."

"I can't believe there are enough Christians in the industry to have a Bible study. How bizarre," Cooper said, still struggling to take in what Jacinta was telling her.

"Oh, you'd be surprised. There are even groups in other cities, too, I think there's one in Miami and Chicago. Look, why don't you come check it out for yourself? We're meeting tonight at seven," Jacinta said, scribbling down an address on the back of a gum wrapper.

Before Cooper could accept or decline the invitation the receptionist told Jacinta that Bob was waiting in his office. Just before ducking inside her booker's tiny office she did manage to quickly call over her shoulder, "See you tonight."

Cooper was stunned. What Jacinta had told her changed how she had thought of modeling, but she only had a minute to process it. While she was still trying to take everything in, Tara popped her head out of her own office and motioned for Cooper to come inside.

"Well, look who finally came to her senses and returned to New York," Tara said as soon as Cooper walked through the door.

Cooper smiled self-consciously.

Tara kissed Cooper once on each cheek before motioning for her to have a seat.

Cooper lowered herself into one of the chairs across from her booker's desk and waited for the onslaught of questions. Tara didn't disappoint her.

"So you've come to tell me you're going to Italy this summer, right? You've had a change of heart and want to be the next Niki Taylor?"

"I think we both know that's not going to happen," Cooper said, stalling for time.

"Maybe not, but if you really worked at it and were willing to put the time in, you could do pretty well," Tara told her.

Cooper was more confused that ever. She'd had qualms about closing the door on her modeling career before meeting Jacinta, and now she was really unsure. What if this was the purpose she was looking for, the reason God allowed her to get into modeling in the first place? She remembered Claire's words from the other day: "I'm sure if you look around, you'll just fall into something." Cooper had definitely fallen into modeling, and now Jacinta had shown her a way to use that.

"Um, Cooper, I'm not boring you am I?" Tara asked, snapping her fingers as if she were trying to bring her young charge out of a trance.

"What? I'm sorry, Tara, I was just thinking."

"Maybe you could share some of those thoughts with me?"

"Well, I came in here convinced that I was going to tell you that there was no way I was going to Italy this summer and that I was done with modeling for good."

"Do I sense a 'but' coming up, or is that just wishful thinking on my part?" Tara asked hopefully.

"No, you're right. I *was* coming in to quit, but now I'm just not sure. You've always known this is not what I want to do forever, but I don't feel like I'm quite done with modeling yet," Cooper explained.

"I'm glad to see this change of heart, but can you give me a little more of a commitment than that?"

"I know, I know. You've been great about letting me take this time off and not bugging me—too much anyway—so here's what I'm thinking. I'm not ready to sign my life away, but I will definitely call Bella as soon as I get back to Seattle and will set something up with them to work during the rest of the school year," Cooper proposed.

"That's a start. And what about Milan?" Tara prompted.

"If I promise to really consider it can I give you an answer at the end of the semester?"

Tara thought for a moment. "I think I can work with that," she said.

"Great then. It looks like we've got a deal."

"One last thing, though. You need to promise to keep in touch and let me know how things are going at Bella. I'll call later this week and let them know you're coming in."

"I'll give you weekly reports," Cooper vowed.

"Good, good," Tara nodded. Then, as if she had been holding back, she enthused, "Oh, girl, I am so excited that you're back! You're not going to regret this."

Cooper hoped she was right. She felt a little apprehensive with everything changing so fast, but is seemed like a fair compromise. She would have two months to see how things went at Bella and could do a lot of praying for guidance between shoots. If she was truly supposed to go to Italy, she was sure it would be made clear to her. After all, she had no doubts about why she had run into Jacinta just before meeting with Tara. God had had a very busy morning.

15

Y ou're going where?" Claire asked when Cooper called her later that afternoon.

"To a models' Bible study," Cooper explained for the third time, then went on to tell her friend all about her exciting morning at Yacomina Models.

"God is so weird the way he does that!" Claire said. "I mean think of all the things that had to happen to bring you to that office this morning: you and Ryan breaking up, your spring break plans getting canceled, you coming home, the only free morning in your schedule being today—thanks to me and Alex—and on and on."

"So you're saying Ryan and I had to break up so I could meet Jacinta and find out about this Bible study and stay in modeling awhile longer?" Cooper bristled.

"I'm not saying you *had* to. I'm just saying that maybe God is making something good come out of a painful situation."

"Okay, I'll give you that. Now I have to go. I want to eat something before Bible study."

"Yeah, I have sewing anyway. Speaking of which, don't forget you have a fitting with me in the morning," Claire reminded her.

"I know and I'll be there. Just don't expect me before noon. This is my vacation, in case you've forgotten."

"Fine. Noon it is, but not a minute later. I don't want to be hemming this dress Friday morning before class."

"I won't be late. I'm anxious to see my one-of-a-kind Claire original anyway. I bet it's gorgeous."

"It may be bragging, but I have to admit it is," Claire said, giggling into the phone.

"See you tomorrow then."

"Tomorrow," Claire agreed. "Oh, and have a good time tonight. Play nice with the other models," she teased.

"Thanks," Cooper answered, her voice dripping with sarcasm. "I'll try my best."

When she entered the old theater off Times Square two hours later, all of Cooper's confidence had drained away. A guard seated at a desk in the lobby looked at her expectantly. Cooper glanced down at the gum wrapper Jacinta had given her. It said "Models for Christ" at the top and had the address. That was all. She hoped she was in the right place.

"I'm here for a Bible study," Cooper lamely explained.

"You want the sixth floor," the guard told her after sizing her up. "A few people are already up there."

Cooper thanked him before getting in an old creaky elevator that made its way slowly to the other floors. When she got out at number six, she found index cards taped to the walls printed with "MFC" and arrows underneath that directed her through several hallways and finally into a small room. Two girls and a guy were setting up folding chairs in a circle. Jacinta wasn't among them.

"Hi, I'm Pascal," said the guy, a blond with a faint accent, when he turned and noticed Cooper standing in the doorway.

He reached out a hand to her and before Cooper could even tell him her name, the girls came over and introduced themselves, too.

Jessica was young-looking with strawberry blond hair and freckles while Melody had dark skin and dark hair swept up under a black beret. Cooper was a little taken aback by their friendliness. She wasn't really used to other models being quite so nice to her. They were usually sort of catty or, if they were nice to her face, she would find out later they had been talking behind her back to the other girls. But these people seemed genuinely nice in the same way Jacinta had that morning.

"So how'd you find out about us?" Melody asked after Cooper had introduced herself.

Cooper briefly told of her association with Yacomina and explained that she had met Jacinta there that morning.

"Well, we're glad you came. I'm sure Jacinta will be here soon enough. We get a lot of people straggling in the first half-hour from shoots that ran over," Melody explained.

Cooper took a seat in one of the gray metal chairs and set her backpack down by her feet. Jessica took the seat next to her, and the two used the time before the meeting to get acquainted. Several others had arrived by the time Melody called things to order, and just as everyone had begun introducing themselves, Jacinta hurried in. She smiled warmly when she saw Cooper and took a seat on the other side of her.

"I'm so glad you came," she whispered, gently squeezing Cooper's arm.

During the introductions Cooper learned that while Jessica and several of the latecomers were models, Melody was a booker for one of the smaller agencies and Pascal was a freelance photographer. When it was her turn, Cooper explained that she was only home on break from school in Seattle and wasn't really sure where her modeling career was going.

"Are you doing anything with Bella out there?" Melody asked. Jacinta started to answer for Cooper, saying she wasn't, when Cooper interrupted.

"Actually, I just decided today that I'm going to start working with them as soon as I get back next week. Jacinta convinced me I needed to see what God might want to do with my modeling career before I quit altogether."

"That's great, Cooper," Jacinta said.

"And I know a few Christian models in Seattle who are signed with Bella," someone else in the group chimed in. "I'll give you their names before you leave tonight."

Cooper was amazed by the warmth and support of these people she had only just met. She couldn't believe they had been here all along. She wished she could rewind the last few years of her life and begin her modeling career again, now that she knew people like this were out there. Well, at least she had found them now.

After opening in prayer, Melody asked if there was anything anyone wanted to discuss before they started the Bible study. A blond girl who's name Cooper couldn't remember spoke up.

"Has anyone else noticed a trend toward women posing with other women in a very suggestive way?" she asked. Several heads bobbed in agreement before she continued.

"Well, I was sent out on this job last week for a women's magazine and they wanted me to practically kiss this other woman. I've dealt with this with guys, where they want to illustrate an article about relationships or something and they ask me to kiss this other model, but this was a new one," she finished.

Several other members of the group told similar stories and Cooper couldn't help being thankful that she hadn't found herself in a similar situation. True, one of her first jobs was for a teen magazine and she was asked if she would kiss one of the male models, but she said she wasn't comfortable with that and it was dropped. She knew from the horror stories she had heard from other models, though, that she had been lucky.

"Did you tell your booker what happened?" Melody asked. The girl admitted she hadn't.

"You really should," Melody continued, "because they really can't ask you to do that without letting you or your booker know that that is what the shoot requires. They were probably just counting on the fact that you'd be too afraid to speak up. Definitely talk to your booker about it."

Wow. Cooper had never thought to tell her booker when she found herself in an uncomfortable situation. One time a photographer and some of the other models had lit up a joint on the way to a shoot out in the country. At the time, Cooper was so stunned she just clammed up. It didn't seem like professional behavior to her, but she didn't know what to say and she was just thankful no one pressured her to join them. After that she made sure all her shoots were local or that she had her own ride there.

The group spent the next forty-five minutes studying and discussing the parable of the talents. Cooper couldn't help feeling the message was picked especially for her. She spent so much time complaining about not being able to make a difference for God, but when He did trust her with opportunities she didn't take them. She buried them instead, just like the wicked servant. But this was a whole new beginning for Cooper, she decided. No more complaining about not having the same gifts Claire or Alex or Emily had. She was going to find a way to make a difference with what she had been given.

During the prayer request time Cooper was surprised again. She expected everyone to be praying that they would get certain jobs or make a lot of money or become more successful, but most of the requests were for people not even at the study. One girl asked for prayer for her booker who had been asking a lot of questions about Christianity lately, another was concerned for a fellow model whose husband had just left her, and another wanted the group to remember to pray for a photographer she had met whose mom had just been diagnosed with cancer.

"So what did you think?" Jacinta asked after the closing prayer and a big group hug.

"I loved it!" Cooper said sincerely. "I wish I could take the whole group back to Seattle with me."

"I know what you mean. I'm going to Milan this summer and it will be really hard to leave everyone."

"You're going to Milan?" Cooper asked, her jaw dropping.

"Yeah, but don't forget, I'll be out in Seattle in the fall for school and our campuses are close enough that we can get together all the time."

"But I'm supposed to go to Milan this summer!" Cooper told Jacinta.

"We may be rooming together then," Jacinta speculated excitedly.

"I haven't decided if I'm going yet, but that would be great!"

"Let me know. Here, I'll write down my address and phone number so you can keep in touch. And look, I know you're just home visiting so I'm sure you have a lot of people to see, but maybe we could get together for coffee before you go back? I'd love to talk to you about Seattle some more and pick your brain about college life."

"Sure, that would be great," Cooper said, writing down her own phone number as well as her home and school addresses.

"Why don't you call me tomorrow and let me know when is good for you," Jacinta proposed.

"I'll do that," Cooper promised.

After that, the group made their way out of the theater and onto 44th Street. A few people turned right, heading toward Sixth Avenue, but everyone else walked toward the 42nd Street subway station in the heart of Times Square. Making their way underground, the group split into those heading uptown or downtown and Cooper followed Jacinta and two others onto a subway platform to wait for a #9 train.

"It would be wonderful if you ended up going to Milan," Jacinta said once they had boarded the train.

"This is the first time I've even considered it seriously. I've been telling Tara 'no way' for the last six months. But yeah, it sure would make it easier knowing someone else who is going."

"I know it's a big decision to make. I'll be praying for you as you try to work it out."

"Thanks. I know it seems so obvious, but I've never really prayed about my modeling career before."

"I'm convinced I wouldn't have a modeling career if I didn't pray about it consistently," Jacinta said.

At her stop Cooper said good-bye to her new friends, then walked slowly home. It had been quite a day and her head was still swimming, but she felt at peace, too. She finally felt like she had a little direction in her life.

When she came in, her mom was sitting at the kitchen table balancing her checkbook. Even at the late hour, her dark hair was perfectly styled in a sleek bob, and she was wearing a sleeveless red blouse with black pants and red ballet flats.

"Hello, sweetheart. How was your day?" she asked without looking up.

"Fine," Cooper answered, wandering into the kitchen and opening several different cupboards in search of a snack.

"I picked up some wonderful raspberries on the way home

tonight if you're hungry, or there's sorbet in the freezer."

"Thanks," Cooper said, scooping up the container of sorbet and grabbing a spoon. She knew she'd finish it off so she didn't bother putting it in a bowl.

"So did you go see Tara today?"

"Yep, I sure did." Cooper answered happily.

Her mother looked up. Apparently she hadn't expected her to be in such a good mood after her meeting at Yacomina.

"What did you end up telling her?"

"Well, I was all set to tell her I was quitting for good, but then the weirdest thing happened. I met this girl and she invited me to a Bible study and she's going to be moving to Seattle in the fall and before I knew it I was telling Tara I'd sign up with Bella in Seattle as soon as I got back and that I'd think about going to Milan this summer."

"So now all of the sudden you want to model again?" her mom asked, obviously confused.

Cooper's face fell. "I thought you'd be happy about my decision."

"Oh, don't misunderstand me, I'm thrilled, but I've been trying to get you to reconsider for months. Now all of the sudden some girl you've never met before invites you to a Bible study and all your plans change?" her mother questioned.

Leave it to Mom to make it sound so ridiculous. It had all made sense when she was explaining it to Claire earlier, why did she have such a hard time communicating with her own mother?

"I've just decided to give it another try, okay?" Cooper stated, rather than asked.

"Of course that's okay. I just don't understand why it's suddenly all different."

Cooper sighed loudly. "It just is," she quietly told her mom before going into her room and shutting the door behind her.

16

"My mom just doesn't get it," Cooper told Claire the next day as she stood in a scarecrow-like position, arms out, wearing the half-finished dress.

"Did you explain it to her the way you explained it to me?" Claire asked.

"Sort of. Oh, I don't know," Cooper breathed in exasperation, dropping her arms to her sides. "Ouch!"

"I told you to keep your arms up. There are pins all down the sides," Claire reminded her unsympathetically.

"Sorry, I forgot, but it's so frustrating. I just don't think my mom would understand if I told her I feel like God wants me to stay in modeling."

"Maybe you need to give her that chance to not understand, though," Claire said gently. "Explain it to her. Then if she doesn't get it, at least you tried. By not even giving her a chance you're not really being fair to her."

"Hey, whose side are you on?" Cooper asked indignantly.

"I'm on the side that doesn't want there to be any sides. I know better than almost anyone how pushy your mom can be, but she's still your mom and I think it bothers you more than you let on that there are all these walls between you."

"I didn't know these fittings included a free therapy session," Cooper joked.

"Laugh if you want, but I really think you need to talk to your mom," Claire persisted.

"I'll think about it. Now can I get out of this thing before I get stuck anymore?"

"I'm just about finished," Claire said. "Okay, there. Take a quick look in the mirror. What do you think?"

"It's magnificent!" Cooper gushed, forgetting about her mom for the time being.

"You really think so?" Claire asked hopefully.

"Of course I do. Donna Karan, watch out!"

"You're the best," Claire said, starting to hug Cooper before crying "ouch!" herself.

"I told you to keep your arms up. There are pins all down the sides," Cooper teased.

"You're such a jerk," Claire responded, rolling her eyes.

Cooper hung around for the rest of the afternoon watching Claire make progress on her dress, then made her way up to her own apartment just before dinnertime. Back in her own bedroom, she suddenly remembered she hadn't called Jacinta yet. Cooper fished the scrap of paper with Jacinta's number on it out of her backpack and grabbed the schedule Alex and Claire had put together for her from her desk, then went in search of the cordless phone. She knew she had called Claire earlier, but had no idea where she left it after that. Eventually she found it next to her blow-dryer in the bathroom. She set both pieces of paper in front of her on her bed and dialed. Jacinta picked it up after only two rings.

"Jacinta? It's Cooper."

"Hey! How are you doing?"

"Great. Just enjoying my vacation. I even got to sleep in today."

"That sounds heavenly. I wish I did."

"You just have to make it a priority like I do. When you start school in the fall, arrange your schedule so you don't have any early morning classes. I highly recommend it," Cooper joked.

"I'll keep that in mind," Jacinta said. "Now what about that coffee date? Do you have any free time this week?"

Cooper glanced down at her schedule. Much to her amazement Thursday was totally open. She was planning to go to the Met or the Guggenheim, but she didn't need to spend all day traipsing through either museum. She could easily meet Jacinta before or after.

"How is tomorrow for you?"

"Oh," Jacinta said, "not too good. I'm going out of town on a shoot and I don't get back until Friday afternoon. When do you fly out?"

"Not until Sunday morning, but my friends have the weekend pretty well tied up. Hey, you could come along, though," Cooper said, the idea just occurring to her. She was sure Jacinta would get along great with Claire and Alex, and it also meant Cooper wouldn't have to feel like a third wheel.

"I don't know. I don't want to mess up your plans."

"Trust me, you wouldn't be messing them up at all. We're going to a movie Friday night and out for coffee afterwards. I'd love to have you come along."

"How about if I just join you for coffee? I'll be tired after that long shoot, and I need to go grocery shopping and do some laundry."

"Ah, the glamorous life of a model!"

"Exactly!" Jacinta said, laughing.

"I understand. Just coffee would be fine, too. We're going to an early movie so how about if you meet us at about nine-thirty?" Cooper proposed. "That should give you time to wash a few loads of clothes."

"I'll be there," Jacinta said, then added, "except I don't know where 'there' is."

"I'm sure we'll go to the Angelika," Cooper said, since the obscure movies Alex picked always seemed to be playing at the artsy little theater near NYU. Other theaters had better popcorn, but the Angelika had personality. "How about if you meet us at Jonathan Morr Espresso? It's just across the street from the theater on that little side street." Cooper and her friends loved Jonathan Morr because it was so huge that it never felt crowded, and they could always find a table, even on Friday night.

"I know the place," Jacinta said. "I'll meet you there."

"Okay, see you Friday night."

As Cooper hung up the phone her father poked his head into her room, making her jump nervously. He was wearing one of seven almost identical charcoal gray suits that were his usual attire. He insisted they were all very different, but Cooper didn't see it. Around his neck he wore a very tame navy tie with little gray flecks. Cooper was always trying to get him to at least try more colorful ties, but he insisted he was set in his ways.

"I didn't hear you come in. You scared me!" Cooper told him.

"Sorry," Mr. Ellis said. "I'll be sure and slam the door really loud next time."

"Very funny. What's up?"

"Your mother called me at the office and said she was tied up. She's going to have to work late so I thought I'd have some Chinese food delivered unless you want to go out."

"No, delivery sounds just fine."

"Mu shu chicken?" her dad queried unnecessarily.

"You got it," Cooper told him, tossing him the phone so he could call their order in. The Chinese takeout restaurant on the corner was programmed into the Ellis's speed dial, they ordered from there so often.

Over dumplings and mu shu Cooper caught her father up on her week.

"So you might go to Milan, huh?" he asked.

"Maybe. I want to take a little time to think about it."

"That sounds wise. It's a big decision. I'm sure you'll make the right choice, though, you always do."

"I'm glad *some*one thinks so," Cooper responded dramatically.

Her dad caught her meaning instantly and frowned a little.

"You're mother thinks so, too. Don't be fooled. If anything, she believes in you too much. She knows how special you are and just doesn't want you to waste the talents you've been given."

"I wouldn't waste them if only I could find them!" Cooper said, before scooping another forkful of rice into her mouth.

"You're finding them, honey. Just be patient. You may need to grow into some of them a bit, that's all."

"Patience never was one of my strong points," Cooper admitted.

"Well that's just one more thing you have to grow into. And another thing. Maybe you could give your mom a break every now and then? You can be a little hard on her sometimes, you know."

She sighed. "That's the second time I've been told that today."

"Maybe you should listen then."

"I know. She's just so hard to talk to sometimes," Cooper complained.

"You have a hard time talking to her because you're so much

alike," her dad explained.

"We are nothing alike! How can you even say that?"

"Because I see the similarities all the time, that's how. For starters, you get your impatience from her. She always wants to be doing something important right now and you're both very hard on yourselves. You both refuse to learn from other people's mistakes. You have to discover everything for yourself. And your sense of adventure certainly doesn't come from me. If it weren't for your mother I doubt I'd ever venture out of New York City, but she lives to explore new places."

"Didn't I get anything from you?" Cooper asked.

"Your hair and your eyes are mine," he told her, "and you definitely got your height from me, but your temperament is all your mother's," he told her with a smile.

"Well I don't see it," Cooper said.

"One day you will. And what's more, you'll be glad. I promise," he told her, stooping to give her a kiss on the forehead before taking his dirty plate over to the sink. "Don't you have any plans with your friends tonight?"

"Nope, I'm all yours. I thought I'd just hang out and do a little reading—something that's not required for once—and relax."

"Sounds good. I think I'm going to watch a little TV."

Once he was in the living room, Cooper's dad called back into the kitchen.

"Did you see you have mail? It's right here on the desk."

Cooper couldn't imagine who would be writing to her at home, but then she remembered she had given Emily her address. She had promised to send Cooper a postcard from Central Oregon while she was at home. Flipping through the stack of mail, Cooper found that she had guessed right. Beneath her fingers was a postcard of a mountain scene with

"Oregon" printed across the top in bold letters, but when she turned it over the writing wasn't Emily's loopy script. It was obviously a guy's writing, and the penmanship was hauntingly familiar. Her eyes scanned down to the bottom of the card, but before she even got to the signature she knew exactly who the card was from. She looked anyway.

At the very bottom were the words "Love, Ryan."

17

Why on earth would he be writing her? And he signed the postcard, "Love, Ryan"? What was that supposed to mean? Cooper was surprised to find that rather than the excitement she expected to feel, she was actually mad. Really mad. After all, she hadn't thought about Ryan once in the last twenty-four hours. And now he just comes barging back into her life with some stupid postcard?

Cooper went back into the kitchen and, leaning against the white countertop, she read:

Dear Cooper,

I bet you're surprised to hear from me, huh? Emily gave me your address. (I had to bribe her with a hot fudge sundae but you're worth it.) I hope you're having a great spring break. Even though mine just started I can already tell it's going to be a really long week. I can't stop thinking about you and wondering if I made the right decision. Maybe I was stupid to give up so soon. Well, I just wanted to let you know that I'm thinking about you and miss you. I hope we can talk when we get back to PCU. See you then. Happy Easter!

Love,

Ryan

Cooper threw the postcard on her desk in disgust. A week ago she would have been thrilled to hear Ryan say he wanted to try again, but something had changed. Cooper had turned a corner and suddenly she didn't know if she wanted to be with Ryan.

Now he wants to give things another chance. Now he wants to work things out. Well maybe it's just too late, Cooper thought smugly. *Maybe I won't be in the mood for a talk when I get back to PCU.*

She picked up her copy of *The Hiding Place,* the paperback Emily had given her for Christmas. It was a true story about a family of Dutch Christians who hid Jews from the Nazis during World War II. This was the first chance Cooper had had to read it and, although it looked really interesting and she wanted nothing more than to lose herself in someone else's life for a while, she just couldn't concentrate. Every time she tried, all the words just blurred together on the page. Finally she put the book down and went out in the living room to watch TV with her dad.

"I thought you were going to read?" he asked when she sank down next to him and Winston Churchill on the couch.

"Eh. I decided I would rather come veg out with you guys," Cooper explained, patting the bulldog affectionately. Her dad was still in his suit and tie.

"I'm honored. We can change the channel if you want," he offered. He was watching the History Channel as usual. Her dad always seemed to be watching either that or CNN. Occasionally she even caught him tuned into C-Span, which she teased him about.

"No, this is fine," Cooper said agreeably. She wasn't planning on paying much attention, anyway.

Cooper was still thinking—and fuming—about Ryan's postcard as she wandered through the Metropolitan Museum of Art the next day. She had slept in and now had the whole day to herself, but it wasn't really hers. Ryan seemed to be following her through the various wings of the museum. She looked at the extensive collection of armor and the medieval art before moving upstairs to her favorite area, the nineteenth century paintings.

Sitting on a bench staring at the Van Goghs, Cooper felt a little more peaceful, and by the time she made her way to the American wing she was even smiling to herself. Peering into one of the fully furnished bedrooms that was corded off, she remembered her conversation with Sam about not visiting the Met in the near future and had to catch herself before she laughed out loud. She bet he was having a great time being back in New York City for spring break. Walking home through the park later that afternoon Cooper was surprised by how much she was enjoying New York herself.

No one was home when she got to the apartment, but her mother had obviously been there because when she dropped her keys on the table in the entryway Cooper noticed a new stack of mail with another Oregon postcard right on top. Her heart stopped beating for at least five seconds, she was sure, and she didn't start breathing normally until she turned it over and saw that it was written in tiny, neat rows of purple ink and had been signed: "Emily."

"Whew," Cooper exhaled and sucked in a breath of clean air.

The postcard was chatty, full of news about how she planned to spend her break—since she had written it on Monday she hadn't actually done much yet—and telling Cooper again how much she wished she had come to Oregon, too. The words were so tiny Cooper had to squint to read them all, but Emily sure managed to cram a lot of information onto the small card. And at the end she had added a P.S.: "I'm really sorry about giving Ryan your address, but he was so insistent. I hope he didn't write anything that upset you." She ended the message with a goofy-looking happy face.

Cooper put this new postcard and the other one in her backpack, tucking them away in the zippered pocket. She wanted to show them to Claire and Alex the next time they were all together and get their opinion.

She saw Alex bright and early the next morning when she met him at the Museum of Radio and Television. *So much for sleeping in,* Cooper grumbled to herself. Alex had called her the night before to make her promise she would be there and as she turned the corner she saw him standing right out front where he said he would be. They said their hellos, paid the admission price, and were inside in a matter of minutes.

"Where to first?" Alex asked as soon as they were through the door.

"I don't know, this was your idea," Cooper reminded him.

"I know. I was just being polite anyway. I have the whole thing planned."

Cooper rolled her eyes at her friend. For as long as she had known him he had always had everything planned. Falling back into their comfortable, old pattern, she found herself following him around the museum. The reason she was so willing to do this, though, was because she had to admit he always made really good plans.

After looking around a bit they selected the programs they wanted to watch and went to a viewing booth where they laughed hysterically for almost two hours at old 60s and 70s sitcoms.

"Look at her hair!"

"Nice sideburns, buddy!"

"Could that miniskirt be any shorter?"

"Guys in platform shoes!"

They gave a running commentary on everything they saw. By the time they left, Alex had several pages of notes for a paper he was writing and Cooper had tears running down her face from laughing so hard. That sort of set the tone for the afternoon. As they headed further downtown in search of something to eat, everything seemed to strike them as funny.

A woman walked by with hair teased into an unnatural style that perfectly resembled one they had just seen on one of the sitcoms at the museum; Cooper only had to glance at Alex and he was laughing again. It took him several minutes to compose himself enough to ask where she wanted to go.

"Anywhere, I'm starving," Cooper answered.

"There are a ton of places by my apartment. Let's head over there and then I can stop by and drop off my notebook."

"Fine with me. It feels good to be out walking, and I've never seen your apartment before."

"You're in for a real treat then."

After unlocking three separate locks, they were finally inside Alex's place. Cooper's eyes darted around the room as she tried to decide where to focus.

The apartment was crammed with all sorts of strange things. A huge cardboard cut-out of Godzilla lived in one corner and someone had added construction paper flames coming out of his mouth. Models of each of the planets in the solar system were hung from the ceiling with fishing line, and there was a Roman column standing in the middle of the room that served absolutely no purpose at all. Every piece of furniture was draped with a blanket or bedspread, no doubt hiding the same kind of ugly upholstery as the couch in Cooper's dorm room.

"I love the idea of having Christmas lights inside," Cooper pointed out, referring to the strings of colored bulbs that framed the windows.

"Thank you. I added that little touch myself," Alex replied.

"We could use your help back at the dorm. That place has no style whatsoever."

"I wasn't really expecting to have anyone over so it's kind of a mess," Alex explained apologetically.

"Not that I don't love it, but how do you tell the mess from the decor?" Cooper teased.

"It's hard at times, but we manage."

Next, Cooper took a quick look into the room Ryan shared with Justin. She was happy to see that it was an even bigger mess than her room was on its worst day. Just as she was about to leave, a photo collage caught Cooper's eye.

"I can't believe you have these out where people can see them!" she yelled to Alex, spying her ninth grade class picture in which she had cut her bangs way too short and another catalog shot of her modeling a dumb-looking sweater with hearts and bows all over it.

"What do I have out?"

"These hideous pictures of me. I thought you were supposed to be my friend?"

"What hideous pictures?" Alex asked, coming up behind her. Then, before she could answer, he saw for himself. "Oh, those," he said with mock casualness.

Cooper could see he was holding back a smile. "And your roommates want to meet me after seeing those?" she asked.

"Are you kidding? *No one* would want to meet you after seeing those," Alex said, breaking into a big smile. "They saw you in that picture of us at graduation. It's right here."

Alex handed Cooper a framed shot of the three friends taken right after their graduation ceremony. Cooper had the same picture in her dorm room.

"They don't even know you're in this collage. They never look at it," Alex continued. "But that gives me an idea. Maybe I should show them these other pictures. That would definitely scare them off."

"Show anyone these pictures and die, Alex, my friend."

"You're so sensitive! Remember, you cut those quarter-inch-long bangs so you would look like Audrey Hepburn. I think it worked...sort of. And, well...it's not like you picked out that sweater yourself."

"Can we just go eat now that you've completely humiliated me?" Cooper asked.

"I'm ready whenever you are," Alex answered, turning toward the door.

When he was safely out in the living room Cooper took the collage and stuffed it under the bed, making sure it was way in the back before grabbing her backpack and joining Alex in the living room.

"Let's eat!" they both said in unison as Alex opened the door and they moved into the hall.

"Jinx! You owe me a Coke," Cooper called.

It was a game they had played for years. Whenever they said the same thing at the same time the first one to yell "jinx" had power over the other one. In junior high the "jinxed" person couldn't talk until someone spoke his name, but at some point during their high school years they upped the ante. At first it had been gum, but now the stakes were a Coke.

"You always call it," Alex complained. "How many Cokes do I owe you now, about twenty six-packs, or what?"

"That sounds about right, and you can start paying up today," Cooper said.

"We'll see."

Once they were on the street, the focus was back on food. "There's a Mexican place over there," Alex said, pointing. "Or there's Italian on that corner, and down the street is a place with good sandwiches and salads."

"Sandwiches and salads, please."

They stepped into the Mayrose Diner on Broadway and took a seat at a table against the window.

"Don't you miss all the weirdness?" Alex asked looking out the window.

"You mean when I'm in Seattle?"

"Yeah, isn't it just too quiet and normal there?"

"No," Cooper answered a little huffily. "Seattle is plenty weird. There's this cool coffee shop downtown called The Sit 'n' Spin that's also a Laundromat, and even New York doesn't have a Toaster Museum," she pointed out, recalling her museum conversation with Sam for the second time in as many days.

'There's a Toaster Museum?" Alex asked, perking up a bit.

"Well, I haven't actually been there, but someone told me about it," Cooper admitted.

"You have to go see it when you get back and give me a full report," Alex said, enthusiastically.

"I'll send you a postcard," she promised.

Their waiter appeared then and Cooper hurriedly looked at the menu before ordering a cobb salad and a large Coke.

"The Coke's on you, don't forget," she reminded Alex.

He just ignored her and placed his order. While they were waiting for their food Alex was describing a film short he was working on for one of his classes.

"It's a time-lapse film of a Chia pet growing," Alex explained.

"We have it set up in a room and we take a picture every fifteen minutes. Then, when all the frames are shown together, it looks like the seeds are sprouting amazingly fast. It's like that film they showed us of clouds in junior high science class where they were just flying across the sky."

"I don't remember watching cloud films in junior high science class," Cooper told him. "And I can't believe you do, but the project sounds neat."

Just then she heard someone saying her name, and it wasn't Alex. She turned around to see where the voice was coming from and standing there holding a takeout bag was Sam.

18

W ha...what are you doing here?" Sam stammered and Cooper blushed, feeling like she'd been caught in a lie. Although she was under no obligation to tell Sam that her spring break plans had changed, she felt awkward about him finding her in New York City.

"Eating lunch," she answered much more casually than she felt.

"I mean what are you doing in New York?" Sam continued, a hint of exasperation creeping into his voice.

"I decided against going to Oregon after all," Cooper explained in a tone that made it clear she wasn't planning to elaborate.

"Oh." Sam clearly wanted to ask more, but he wisely didn't. Cooper was still so surprised to run into Sam that she just stared at him. As usual his hair was falling in his eyes. Only when Sam began shifting his weight from foot to foot uncomfortably did Cooper realize there were introductions to be made.

"I'm sorry! Sam, this is Alex. Alex, Sam," Cooper managed

to get out. Turning to Alex she explained, "Sam goes to PCU, too. He's the one who told me about the Toaster Museum."

Before Cooper could say more Alex had invited Sam to join them and was firing questions at him.

"So what are you studying? How did you meet Cooper? Do you honestly like Seattle better than New York?"

Sam answered easily, explaining that he was studying broadcasting, as it was the closest thing PCU had to film production. He told Alex that he had met Cooper in line at registration and that he was dying to get back to New York, having left against his will in the first place. Even though he was talking to Alex, though, Cooper noticed that Sam's eyes met hers more than they met her friend's. Feeling self-conscious, she tried meeting his gaze, hoping it would make him look away. Instead, he just smiled warmly and kept watching her while he spoke.

"So do I pass?" Sam joked when he was done responding. "That felt sort of like a test."

"Yep. You gave me all the right answers," Alex told him.

Just when Cooper was sure Sam was about to leave, Alex did the unforgivable.

"Hey, if you're not busy tomorrow night why don't you join us for a little video party? We're getting together at my apartment around seven, and I live right around here."

Cooper's eyebrows shot up. What was Alex thinking? There was no way she was going to spend a whole night squirming under Sam's penetrating gaze, explaining why she wasn't in Oregon after all.

"Thanks, but I can't," Sam replied. Cooper hadn't realized she had been holding her breath until it all came rushing out in a whoosh. Alex looked at her a little strangely but she just glared back at him. He obviously didn't get Cooper's strong hint, though.

"C'mon," he persisted. "If you have plans with someone else already, just bring them along."

"I'd really like to, but I do already have plans and unfortunately they're with someone I can't bring along. My little sister is in the hospital and as much as I'm sure she'd enjoy it, I don't think her doctor will let her out for a video party."

"Oh, that's too bad," Alex said, nodding sympathetically.

A wave of guilt washed over Cooper at Sam's reminder of his sick sister. She couldn't believe she had been so selfish about Alex inviting him to join their little party.

"How's your sister doing?" Cooper asked, attempting to quiet her conscience.

"She's having kind of a rough week, actually. She's going to have to start chemo treatments again and her hair had just grown back in from the last time so, understandably, she's a little bummed," he explained.

"I bet she's glad you're home though," Cooper added, trying to lighten his mood. Her plan backfired, though.

"That's another thing," Sam began saying animatedly. "I'm only home for a week and Rachel—that's my sister—really needs me. But my mom has forbidden me to go to the hospital tomorrow until evening, even though she'll be at work all day! She thinks I need to get out, so Rachel is going to be stuck in that stupid hospital all day and I'll be wandering around the city, miserable!"

It was as if a dam had broken and a torrent of words just kept flowing out of Sam's mouth. Suddenly, he seemed to remember where he was. Looking across the table first at Cooper then at Alex he started apologizing.

"I'm really sorry. I don't know why I'm laying all of this on you. I should probably go anyway. My sister's waiting for her lunch," he explained, motioning to the brown paper takeout bag he had set down on the table. Then he added "the cobb salad from here is her favorite," giving a little shrug.

"Don't worry about unloading. That's what friends are for," Alex told Sam, before Cooper could think of anything to say.

Never mind the fact that they just met today so they're hardly friends, Cooper was thinking, when Alex did it again.

"Anyway, you don't have to worry about your sister. Cooper can spend the day with her tomorrow," Alex volunteered. At the mention of her name Cooper's eyebrows shot up again— the way the conversation was going, she thought she might as well just freeze her expression that way—as she couldn't believe the words coming out of Alex's mouth. To her further amazement he just kept going.

"She has nothing better to do anyway, really. I'd offer myself, but I have plans. So there, problem solved. Aren't you glad you ran into us?"

Sam seemed almost as stunned as Cooper by the offer. Almost. He started to protest that it really wasn't necessary and he couldn't let her give up her last day in New York to spend it with someone she didn't even know, but Cooper could see that he didn't mean it. He was clearly relieved at the thought and she knew she couldn't back out now. Besides, Sam was looking at her with such gratitude, his gold eyes shining brightly, that she didn't have the heart.

"Don't worry about it," Cooper said. "Alex is right. I didn't really have anything planned and I'd love to meet your sister. Just tell me when to be there."

"Oh, man, you don't know what a relief this is to me. She's at Sloan-Kettering and pretty much any time after eleven is good," Sam said, actually smiling for the first time since she ran into him.

"Why don't you write all that down for me and give me a

room number, too," Cooper said, pushing a paper napkin toward him and fishing in her purse for a pen.

Sam wrote down all the pertinent information then stood before handing it back to Cooper. Grabbing his sister's lunch off the table and his jacket from the chair back he said his good-byes, thanking them both again several times. Then instead of turning to go he bent over and kissed a shocked Cooper on the cheek before racing out the door. When he was gone Cooper leaned forward in her chair.

"You're dead meat," she said to her smiling friend.

"What?" Alex asked with mock-innocence. "What did I do?"

"Just eat your lunch," Cooper told him with disgust. Their meals had arrived just as Sam was hurrying down the street outside.

"Sam seems like a very nice young man," Alex continued, adopting a fatherly tone. "What do you know about his future plans?"

Cooper took a bite of salad and rolled her eyes at Alex. She spent the rest of the time at the restaurant trying to figure out how she was going to entertain a hospital-bound little girl she had never even met. The thought made her stomach tighten.

Cooper still hadn't completely forgiven Alex when they met Claire at her apartment later before the movie, but at least now she had someone else to talk to.

"My teacher *loved* the dress!" Claire announced before even saying hello.

"Oh, Claire, that's wonderful! I'm so proud of you!" Cooper told her. Alex twirled his girlfriend around before pulling her close for a kiss.

"I wouldn't kiss him if I were you," Cooper told Claire. "He's been a brat all day."

"How is that different from any other day?" Claire teased.

"I see your point, but this was definitely worse than usual," Cooper said. "Go ahead, Alex. Tell Claire how I'll be spending my last day in New York?"

Both girls looked expectantly at Alex, and Cooper was glad to see he at least had the decency to squirm a little when put on the spot. He recovered quickly, though.

"Well you know how Cooper was complaining about not having any ministry opportunities?" Alex began. "I simply found a way for her to make a difference by visiting a poor, sick little girl at the hospital tomorrow." After a short pause he added, "And if that little girl happens to have an older brother who can't stop drooling over our little Cooper, so much the better, right?"

Claire turned to Cooper and waited for the rest of the story. She didn't have to wait long.

"You remember Sam, the quasi-annoying guy from PCU that I mentioned? Well he's actually a pretty nice guy, but that's another story. Anyway, we ran into him today downtown and he was all upset because his sister, who has leukemia, is in the hospital and she's going to be all alone tomorrow. After inviting him to join us for videos tomorrow night, Alex kindly offered my services—without consulting me, of course—so I'm hanging out at Sloan-Kettering for the afternoon." The explanation came out in a rush without a single pause for breath.

Claire just looked from Cooper to Alex and back again. When she still hadn't spoken after several seconds, Cooper took another verbal swipe at her offending friend.

"And he was *not* drooling," she added. "You have an over-active imagination."

"Well he didn't kiss *me* good-bye now, did he?" Alex shot back. Then, turning to Claire, he reported that Sam couldn't keep his eyes off Cooper.

"He kissed you?" Claire asked. "You didn't mention that."

"And she blushed," Alex added triumphantly.

"I did not. He was just grateful. You take that back," Cooper demanded.

At that Claire began laughing uncontrollably.

"It's not funny," Cooper wailed, sinking into a chair in defeat. She had been sure Claire would be on her side in this.

"It's just that...that this is just like...like in junior high!" Claire managed to get out between laughs. By now tears were streaming down her face as well.

At that Alex started laughing, too.

"You're right," he said. "It's just like when Cooper and I first met. She was going to beat me up because I told that guy who sat in front of her in history class that she liked him."

"This is nothing like junior high," Cooper maintained. She tried to sound stern, but in spite of herself she began to smile the tiniest bit.

"Remember?" Claire asked. "You made me come with you to follow Alex home and confront him after school that day?"

"Well Alex had no right telling some stupid boy I liked him when he didn't even know me," Cooper said, still indignant over the long-ago incident.

"But you *did* like that boy in your history class," Claire reminded.

"Yeah, didn't he start talking to you and passing you notes after that?" Alex chimed in. "Maybe after you go visit Sam's sister, he'll start passing you notes, too. Is he in your history class?"

"He's in my photography class," Cooper answered, "but that is *so* not the point," she added in a frustrated tone. Before she could stop herself, though, she was wondering what Sam might say if he did write her a note.

"I agree that Alex was wrong to just volunteer you like that," Claire said, "but it doesn't sound like his sole motive was embarrassing you like it was in junior high, so that's progress, isn't it? And visiting a sick kid in the hospital, how can you say no to that?"

"I can't. Or Alex can't anyway," Cooper agreed.

"You know I'd go with you, but I've got the grandparents coming over, and it will be hard enough to escape tomorrow night," Claire said sympathetically.

"And I'm working on my film short," Alex added, not seeming any too sorry that he wouldn't be able to join her.

"So how am I going to entertain this little girl I don't even know?" Cooper asked.

"We'll think of something," Claire said.

They were still thinking as they stood in line for tickets at the Angelika Film Center. Looking across Houston Street Cooper prayed for some sort of divine inspiration, that God would just zap her with some brainstorm, but she was still drawing a blank as she entered the dark theater.

Cooper felt much better after focusing on the story on the big screen for two hours. As they crossed over to Jonathan Morr, she reminded Claire and Alex that Jacinta was joining them.

"So try to be on your best behavior, okay, Alex?" she warned. "And in case you're unsure what qualifies as good behavior, let me spell it out for you: No showing embarrassing pictures of me, no asking her if she has any available friends to set me up with, and no volunteering me for anything. You got it?"

"Your wish is my command," he answered.

Somehow, this didn't put Cooper at ease, but when Jacinta showed up about twenty minutes later, Alex kept his word. Over several cappuccinos each, they talked about modeling and fashion and film so everyone was included in the conversation, and Jacinta hit it off with Claire and Alex, no problem. In fact, before they left, Claire asked for Jacinta's number so they could be sure to stay in touch.

It wasn't until they were walking to the subway that the hospital visit came up again. Cooper asked Alex what she could bring the next night when they watched videos, then couldn't resist adding, "I'll have to pick it up on my way home from the *hospital*, though," making sure to really emphasize the word hospital.

"Why don't you pick up some drinks?" he suggested, seeming to ignore her little dig.

"The hospital?" Jacinta questioned. "Is someone you know sick?"

"Well it's not exactly someone I know," Cooper began, then filled Jacinta in on the whole story.

"That's a strange situation all right. Do you want some company? I have a few free hours in the afternoon and it might be less awkward with someone else there."

"Yes!" Cooper practically shouted, giving Jacinta a hug. "That would be great!"

"You're more than welcome to come watch videos tomorrow night with us, too. I just don't know how much of us you can take in one weekend," Cooper laughed.

"I have plans tomorrow night, but I'll definitely meet you at the hospital. In front of Sloan-Kettering at noon." Jacinta repeated.

"That's the plan. Have I told you you're the best?" Cooper asked Jacinta as they descended the steps into the subway station.

"Several times," Jacinta answered, " but feel free to keep the compliments coming."

19

As she made her way to the hospital on Saturday morning, Cooper realized that in less than twenty-four hours she would be on her way back to Seattle. It seemed impossible; college and her PCU friends felt so far away. When she had gone to her grandparents' in Connecticut for Christmas that had felt more like a vacation; her heart never really left Seattle on that trip and she couldn't wait to get back. But this was different. She was finally growing to love New York City after all these years, or maybe she was just realizing how much she had always loved it. It would be harder to leave this time. She felt like she fit in more than she ever had in the past, but now she fit in at PCU, too. It felt strange to belong so wholly to two completely different worlds.

Cooper was running a few minutes late, as usual, so Jacinta was standing out front when she got to Sloan-Kettering. In the elevator on the way up to Rachel's room, Cooper showed Jacinta all the things she had stuffed into her bag before leaving her apartment that morning.

"I just have no idea how we're going to pass a whole afternoon," Cooper said, beginning to worry all over again. "But at least I came prepared. I have magazines, felt pens, colored paper, scissors, Play-doh, glue sticks, Trivial Pursuit cards, candy...." Cooper listed off.

"Are you sure you brought enough?" Jacinta said, a hint of a smile turning up the corners of her mouth.

Cooper leaned against the wall of the elevator, her body sagging under the weight of the pressure she was feeling. "I know, I'm totally going overboard, but I was awake most of last night trying to imagine what it must be like to be ten years old stuck in a hospital bed for weeks on end. I mean, if I were Rachel, what could some dumb friend of my brother's bring that would take my mind off that for an afternoon?"

"Well, when you put it that way, I think we better run down to the gift shop for some more stuff," Jacinta said. "I wasn't depressed until just now, you know."

"Sorry. I just know I won't know what to say to her. I thought if we could stay busy, maybe she won't notice."

When they got off the elevator, Cooper glanced down at the slip of paper Sam had given her to double-check Rachel's room number.

"I think it's right down here," Cooper told Jacinta as she led the way down a long corridor. Before she was ready, they had reached the door to Rachel's room. Cooper took a deep breath, whispered a quick prayer, and pushed the door open.

"Are you Rachel?" she asked the girl with dark hair and pale skin sitting on the far bed. The question was unnecessary, though. She had those same intense gold eyes that Sam did, but hers seemed even bigger than her brother's because the rest of her was so small.

"Which one of you is Cooper?" the girl asked, putting down the hand-held video game she had been playing and carefully studying the two strangers in her room.

"I am," Cooper answered. She moved across the room so Rachel could get a better look, feeling like a lab specimen.

"Oh," the little girl replied, then just sat there quietly on top of the stark white hospital sheets.

"So your brother told you I was coming, huh?" Cooper asked.

"Of course, but I thought there would only be one of you."

"Oh, sorry. This is my friend Jacinta. I was afraid I might not be fun enough all on my own so she came with me. I hope that's okay," Cooper explained. Jacinta gave a meek little wave from the doorway as if to back up her friend's story. She had come from a job that morning and was carrying her rather bulky modeling book under her other arm.

"So you go to school with my brother?" Rachel asked.

"Yep. We even have a photography class together."

"Sam's out taking pictures for his photography class right now." Rachel looked at Cooper carefully. "So what are you doing here anyway?" she asked.

Cooper was surprised by the little girl's directness but recovered quickly and with confidence managed to say, "Visiting you!" as if she dropped in on young cancer patients every day of the week. As she spoke, she sat down on the corner of Rachel's bed. It seemed a little intrusive, but the girl was so small, she barely took up the top half of the bed herself.

"I know you're visiting me," Rachel said, "but why?" It was clear Cooper wasn't going to get off the hook quite so easy.

Cooper thought for a moment. She knew she couldn't very well reply, "I don't have any idea what I'm doing here," even though that was what she was thinking.

"Because your brother asked me to?" she answered, Jeopardy-style. She prayed her response would satisfy Rachel as she really didn't know what else to say.

"You really didn't have to, you know. Sam thinks I can't be by myself, but when he's away at school I'm by myself a lot because our mom can't always take time off from work just because I'm sick."

Cooper considered this for a moment. "Oh, I think your brother knows you can take care of yourself just fine. But I think he wanted me to meet you. I don't have any sisters of my own so maybe he was just trying to share you with me," she said.

"I guess that makes sense," Rachel finally agreed. "And if you ever need a brother you can borrow Sam anytime."

Cooper laughed. "He might not like being loaned out, though. Maybe you should check with him."

"No, he won't mind because he really likes you," Rachel reported matter-of-factly.

"Did he say that?" Cooper questioned, wondering just what Sam had told his sister.

"Yeah, he said you were nice, but he told me not to talk too much about New York because it makes you mad."

"I can't believe he said that!" Cooper replied indignantly. Then turning to Rachel she said soothingly, "You can talk about anything you want. It's just your brother who has to watch it."

"Do we have to talk? I'd rather do something."

"That's even better. You know, I brought a few things with me...well, actually more than a few things," Cooper explained, grinning sheepishly at Jacinta, who had joined them at the bed. "Wanna take a look?"

Rachel nodded eagerly so Cooper turned her backpack upside down and dumped the contents out on the bed, causing several markers and cans of Play-doh to spill to the floor. The little girl began examining some of the items, commenting from time to time.

"I have my own markers that change colors when you use this other pen on them. It's called a magic pen, but it's not really magic, just some special chemicals in the ink, I think," she explained, then chirped, "Hey, that rhymed!"

Rachel liked the Trivial Pursuit cards, too. They quizzed each other for quite a while, keeping track of who had the most correct answers, then Rachel wanted to look through magazines.

"I don't have anything but fashion magazines," Cooper explained. "I thought maybe we could cut them up, though, and glue pictures or words to the construction paper."

Rachel seemed to consider the proposal. "I might make a card for my brother later if that's okay with you."

"That'd be fine with me."

"What's that book you have?" Rachel suddenly asked Jacinta.

"Oh, you mean this one? It's my modeling book. It's just a bunch of boring pictures of me."

"Oooh! Can I see? I didn't know you were a model," Rachel said, newfound admiration in her voice. "Do you know Cindy Crawford?"

"No," Jacinta laughed. "I'm afraid I don't. But Cooper's a model, too. We're with the same agency."

"I don't know Cindy Crawford, either," Cooper said before Rachel could ask.

"Sam didn't tell me any of this when he said you were coming."

"I don't think your brother knows I've done any modeling and Sam's never met Jacinta so...." Cooper let her explanation trail off.

"Why doesn't he know?" Rachel asked. "If I were a model, I'd be sure everyone knew."

"I guess it's not a big deal to me. Anyway, I don't want people to like me just because I'm tall and have good cheekbones so I can make money getting my picture taken. I want them to like me for other more important reasons."

"But I still wouldn't mind being pretty," Rachel said. The girl's words tugged at Cooper's heart.

"Oh, Rachel. You *are* pretty," Cooper reassured her. "You have the most incredible eyes...." She smiled at the child. "I know it's hard to feel good about your looks when you're sick, but you really are a beautiful girl. Don't ever forget that, okay?"

Rachel nodded.

After that, they looked at Jacinta's pictures and Rachel was amazed at how different she looked in each one. Several times when they turned the page she would insist, "That isn't you!" and look from the book to Jacinta, searching for the resemblance.

"It's amazing what they can do with a little make-up, isn't it?" Jacinta asked.

"It sure is," Rachel agreed.

"Just remember that when you see all those beautiful women in the magazines, Rachel. When they're not working and they don't have someone to do their hair and make-up, they look just like me."

Rachel looked at Jacinta with her hair pulled back and her clean-scrubbed face without a trace of make-up on it and seemed to be considering whether or not to believe her.

"It's true, Rachel, really," Cooper agreed.

"Hey, I've got a way to prove it to you," Jacinta said. "What if we can do the same thing for you? I'll make a deal with you: When you get out of the hospital, I'll set up a fashion shoot for you, as long as your mom says it's okay."

Rachel's eyes lit up at the proposal, but Cooper was a little concerned. She shot Jacinta a questioning look.

"Now, it won't be a real modeling job, you understand. But we can take the pictures and make you your own book from them. I'm sure my friends from Bible study will help. Pascal can take the pictures and Melody has a friend who can do your make-up."

Cooper began to understand what Jacinta meant at last. Of course Pascal and Melody would help. It was perfect! Cooper began getting into the planning, too, but then Rachel's face fell.

"But what if I lose my hair right before the pictures are taken?" she asked, her voice rising noticeably. "I was a mess when I got out of the hospital last time."

"The offer's good anytime," Cooper said as Rachel's expression became one of resignation. Then an idea struck her. "Wait a minute, Rachel. Haven't you ever seen any bald models?" she asked. "Several very beautiful models shave their heads on purpose, and they have no problem getting work, even without hair."

"Some of them do even better that way," Jacinta joined in.

"Really?" Rachel asked a little hopefully.

"Really," Cooper answered. "I bet we can even find some of them in these magazines I brought. Let's take a look."

"First one to find one wins!" Rachel shouted and they all began furiously paging through the publications.

They were able to find not just one but four shots of models with little or no hair, and Rachel carefully cut each of the pictures out and stuck them up over her bed. After a while, Jacinta looked at her watch then jumped up.

"I was supposed to leave thirty minutes ago!" she explained, hurrying to gather up her things. Grabbing her coat, her purse, and her book she quickly said her good-byes, but not before writing her name and number down for Rachel.

"Now you don't forget to call me when they let you out of here," Jacinta reminded. "And don't forget to ask your mother either."

"I won't," Rachel called from her spot on the bed.

Once Jacinta was gone, Cooper and Rachel cleaned up the mess they had made throughout the afternoon. When Sam came in an hour later they were watching cartoons and seeing who could make the best Play-doh person. Cooper's figure ended up looking more like a cat than a person. Rachel's had a blue face and was bald, but it also had a huge Play-doh smile and Cooper declared it the winner.

"It's pretty quiet in here," Sam said, crossing the room to give Rachel a hug. He looked at Cooper questioningly. Cooper told herself he must merely be wondering how the day went, but she couldn't help feeling like he might be looking for something more in her eyes.

"We're just winding down from earlier," Cooper explained, averting her gaze.

"Yeah," Rachel chimed in. "Cooper's friend is going to make me into a model. For a day anyway."

"What?" Sam asked.

"Uh, I hope that's okay." Cooper quickly explained, giving Sam all the pertinent details. "It's just for fun and Rachel is under strict orders to talk to your mother about it first."

"And even if I don't have any hair, that's okay, because look..." Rachel told Sam, pointing to the pictures above her bed. "A lot of models are bald these days."

Sam gave Cooper a quizzical look, but she just smiled at him.

"I have Jacinta's phone number right here," Rachel said, holding up a sheet of pink construction paper.

"She's really nice, and it would just be some friends of hers from a modeling industry Bible study doing the shoot," Cooper added.

"And how do you know these people?"

"Oh, Cooper's a model, too," Rachel said. "She didn't tell you because she didn't want you to like her just because she's tall and gets her picture taken."

"What is she talking about?" Sam asked while Cooper turned bright red.

"Nothing really. I've done a little modeling, that's all."

It was obvious that Sam was confused by all the information Rachel had just given him, but he wisely let the matter go, changing the subject altogether.

"Don't you have a party to go to?" he asked Cooper.

She looked down at her watch and couldn't believe how late it was. She hoped Alex and Claire were running late. The afternoon had gone so fast and she realized that she had been worried for nothing. Rachel had actually entertained her rather than the other way around.

"You're right, I need to get going," she told Sam. "And as for you," Cooper said, addressing Rachel this time, "you hurry up and get out of this hospital, okay? And tell Jacinta I want copies of some of those pictures when they're done." Then before leaving she added her own name and address to the paper where Jacinta's was scrawled and pulled the candy she had brought out of her backpack.

"If you write me at school I promise to write back," Cooper said from the doorway of Rachel's hospital room. "And don't let your brother eat all this candy before you get any." Then with a quick wave she was gone.

She was already halfway down the hall when she heard Sam call out, "Cooper, wait."

She turned and found him jogging toward her.

"I just wanted to say thanks again for coming today. You don't know what a relief it was to know she wasn't just sitting here bored all day. She's been so disappointed because I had promised to take her all over the city when I came home and then she got sick again, but she really seems to like you," Sam explained, giving Cooper's arm a squeeze. And even though she willed herself not to feel anything, the spot where his fingers were became all tingly. Sam didn't seem to notice her reaction, though, because he just continued talking.

"My mom was wrong about me needing a break from the hospital, but I think maybe Rachel needed a break from me. I haven't seen her smile this much all week."

"I'm sure it has nothing to do with needing a break from you," Cooper assured him, struggling not to focus on his hand which was still holding her arm. "She talks about you all the time. She's really great."

"Still, I'm sure you could have found a better way to spend your last day in New York."

"Actually, I don't think I could have," Cooper told Sam. "I'll see you back at school, huh?"

"Yeah, see you Monday," Sam said.

She started walking away for the second time when he said "Oh, and Cooper? Just for the record I'd like you even if you weren't tall, so you don't have to worry."

When Cooper turned back, he was just standing there, smiling.

20

L et me in," Cooper yelled through the door when she arrived at Alex's apartment. "I come bearing beverages and they're heavy, so open the door before my arms break off!"

"Sorry, my hands were all gross," Claire said, wiping a glob of something off her lime green dress. "I'm trying to make cookies, but this kitchen is a joke. They have one mixing bowl, no measuring cups or spoons, and I sent Alex out for new cookie sheets since the only one they have is covered with rust."

"Mmmm! Sure am glad I brought my appetite," Cooper responded sarcastically.

"Don't worry, we're still ordering pizza and the guys always have a cupboard full of microwave popcorn, so that's an option, too."

"Okay, I feel better then. I'm glad I'm not late anyway."

Alex burst through the door just then, loaded down with purchases. He pulled two new cookie sheets, a measuring cup, and a set of measuring spoons from one bag, and a large plastic sack of ice from the other.

"They don't have any ice cube trays either," Claire whispered.

"You're quite the little housekeeper, aren't you?" Cooper teased as Alex stashed the ice in the freezer.

"What can I say? I'm not real big in the culinary arts," Alex shot back. "And how is our own little Florence Nightingale? Back from tending the sick so soon?"

"You're such a jerk," Cooper answered, punching him in the arm.

"Seriously, how did it go?" Claire asked, giving Alex a stern look.

"It went really well," Cooper reported soberly. "She's such a sweet little girl and she was so easy to hang out with."

"And her brother's with her now?" Claire asked.

"Mmm-hmm," Cooper answered nodding her head. "And their mom will be there later."

"I'm glad it went okay," Claire told her.

"So am I," Alex agreed. "Did you get any green Jell-O or tapioca pudding while you were there? I wanted to have a hospital theme for our menu tonight but Claire nixed that idea."

"No, I didn't have any Jell-O, green or otherwise," she told Alex in an exasperated tone then turned to Claire and said, "and thank *you* for taking over the menu planning." Claire just shook her head.

Reaching into another bag Alex pulled out two videos before announcing, "And the theme for tonight is movies set in—or mentioning the city of—Seattle! And I want you to know this was a hard one, so I hope you appreciate all the trouble I went to," he told Cooper.

Halfway into the first movie, the trio had finished off most of the pizza and a bag of popcorn and were eating cookie dough straight from the bowl when one of Alex's roommates came in.

"Hey, Justin, you're just in time. We saved you a piece of

166

pizza," Alex said, locating a lone slice under a pile of napkins and other debris.

The girls looked at each other and made a face, but Justin gratefully took the food from Alex and wasted no time devouring it before popping another bag of popcorn in the microwave.

"Does anybody want anything to drink while I'm up?" he asked. Of course, everyone did.

After that interruption everyone settled back down to watch the rest of the movie, not moving again until the credits rolled. It wasn't until then that Alex finally introduced Cooper to his roommate.

As she and Justin were saying awkward hello's, Cooper heard Alex mention something about pictures and she quickly excused herself to follow him into his room.

"Looking for something?" she asked innocently as he searched his desk for the collage.

"What did you do with it?" Alex asked.

"Do with what?"

"You know very well what."

Cooper leaned in the doorway, refusing to say a word. Finally, when she was convinced that Alex wouldn't be finding the embarrassing pictures of her, at least not that night, she went back out to the living room. He was still threatening to get even with her later that night when she said good-bye.

"When I find those pictures I'm going to have them blown up poster-size and wallpaper my room with them," Alex threatened.

"Go right ahead," Cooper told him, certain he'd never really go to all that trouble.

On the curb in front of his building a few minutes later, though, they were the best of friends again.

"It looks like this is it," Cooper announced while Claire flagged down a taxi for the two of them. The subway was still running, but they had promised their mothers they wouldn't ride it that late at night.

"I can't believe you're going back already," Alex said. "Are you sure you don't want to transfer somewhere a little closer to home?"

"Don't tempt me. It's hard enough leaving you guys as it is."

"Good. It should be," Alex said, showing no mercy.

Claire had been successful and the cab was waiting so Cooper quickly hugged Alex and said good-bye. During the ride uptown, a few tears slid down Cooper's cheeks and for just a minute she wondered if maybe she shouldn't consider transferring after all. But then she tried to imagine not rooming with Emily or hearing Kenzie and Chris play at The Cup or being a part of Allie's crazy schemes...and she couldn't picture it. She belonged at PCU.

Just when she was starting to feel better, they arrived at their apartment building and Cooper had to say good-bye to Claire, which was even harder. They paid the cabdriver and rode the elevator upstairs like death row prisoners being led to their execution. At Claire's floor Cooper held the "door open" button while they hugged and cried.

"You better come home this summer, that's all I have to say," Claire called out as the elevator door closed.

Once in her own bedroom, the exhaustion finally hit Cooper and she sprawled across her bed, staring at the ceiling for a full twenty minutes before she even had enough energy to undress and get under the covers. And she only did that after Winston Churchill sprawled across her stomach, forcing her to move. Packing would have to wait until morning.

Unfortunately, Cooper didn't have much more energy when

her mom woke her just after eight.

"Cooper, honey, time for breakfast. I made French toast," she heard her mom saying through a sleepy fog.

"Huh?" she answered, wiping her eyes and trying to remember what day it was. Then, sitting up in bed it all started coming back to her. She would be on a flight to Seattle in just a few hours. Spring break was over.

She stumbled down the hall and made her way to the kitchen table where there was indeed French toast waiting. The delicious smell alone almost made it worth getting up so early. Almost.

"Did you have fun with your friends last night?" her father asked between bites. "You were watching videos at Alex's, right?"

"Yeah. It was nice. Hard to say good-bye, though."

"I bet. But it will be summer soon enough."

"True, but I still don't know where I'll be this summer," Cooper explained.

"I'm sure you'll at least be able to get together with your friends for some part of the break," her dad assured her.

After finishing her breakfast Cooper knew she couldn't put off packing any longer. She pulled out her suitcase and began stuffing inside everything in sight. It wasn't until she was almost done that she remembered she was still in her pajamas and would need something to wear on the plane so she pulled several pieces of clothing out of her bag and set them on the edge of her bed while she went to shower. A short time later she slipped a short black knit dress over her head then topped it with a satiny silver blouse that she tied at her waist instead of buttoning. She stuffed her make-up and still-wet toothbrush into her bag, then strapped on her clunky black sandals, one of which had to be retrieved from under her desk, and she was ready to go.

In the cab on the way to the airport she was finally able to relax a little. She had said good-bye to her father back at the apartment, but her mother had insisted on riding out to the airport with her so they sat side by side, zooming toward Queens.

"I can't believe your visit's over so fast. It seems like you just got here," Mrs. Ellis lamented. "Do you feel ready to go back to school?"

"A little," Cooper admitted. "I'm anxious to see my friends." It felt awkward trying to make conversation with her mother, but Cooper was sort of glad for the company and she had to admit she felt a little sad to be leaving New York this time.

"At least you were able to get your mind off Ryan for a while, weren't you?" her mom asked, smiling encouragingly.

"As a matter of fact, I was. I haven't thought about him at all these last few days." It was only then that Cooper remembered she had never even remembered to bring up the whole post-card thing with Alex and Claire. "I think I'm pretty much over him," Cooper said confidently. She hoped she would still feel as confident when they were in the same time zone.

"I'm glad to hear that," her mom said, patting Cooper's arm. "I know it's bound to happen, but still it's very difficult as a mother to watch your daughter get hurt. As irrational as it is, if I could I think I would lock you away in your room until you were forty to keep you safe, but I know I can't."

"No, thankfully, you can't," Cooper said, staring at her mother in disbelief. "So don't even think about it."

"Just wait until you're a mother," her mom cautioned. "Growing up, I swore I would never do the things my mother did, but I find myself doing them all the time. And you're so much like I was at your age, so headstrong and wanting to make a difference in the world…it worries me."

"I'm not headstrong," Cooper protested, crossing her arms in front of her.

Her mother snorted. "You are the most headstrong girl I've ever seen! I've all but given up offering advice because I know that anything I suggest, you'll only do the opposite, so why bother?"

"That's not true! I don't make decisions just to spite you, I just want different things than you do," Cooper explained.

"Honey, I'm not trying to pick a fight. Honest. I just want you to know that I miss you and I believe in you and I wish you didn't have to go to school so far away."

"But I thought you were okay with me going to PCU." Cooper said.

"You didn't let me finish," her mother said. "I was about to say 'but I understand.' I wanted nothing more than to get away from home when I was your age and find a life of my own. I don't have a problem with that, I just hope that whatever life you find, I can be a part of it."

"Of course you'll always be a part of my life…even if you drive me crazy sometimes," Cooper explained, leaning against her mom's shoulder. It was funny how Cooper could feel so defensive one minute then so loved the next, but she and her mom were always that way with each other. Maybe her dad was right. They were alike in that way, anyway.

"Glad to hear it, sweetheart," her mom said, patting Cooper's shoulder. "Now, Penny will be waiting for you at the airport, won't she?"

"That's what she said when she and Brian dropped me off at the airport, on their way out of town."

At the terminal, Cooper said her final good-bye and headed forlornly inside. She wasn't ready to leave yet. Sometimes it felt so good to be on her own, but at other times it sure was nice to be someone's little girl.

On the plane she still couldn't shake the feeling of loneliness. When she left for college in the fall, Cooper had been ecstatic the whole way there. So why was she feeling so homesick now?

As she landed in Seattle, the sky was typically gray. Strangely enough, this made Cooper suddenly perk up. It felt good to be back in Seattle, and she couldn't wait to see her roommate. She and Emily were so different, but they were a good balance for each other, and she missed their late night talks. Cooper had thanked God many times for whoever it was in the housing office that had linked them up as roommates. She couldn't wait to hear all about Kenzie's and Allie's spring break either.

Making her way to the baggage claim, though, she was glad it was her aunt and not her friends who were picking her up because she knew they would go out of their way to embarass her, especially Allie. After Christmas break they had all gone to the airport to pick up Kenzie and Ethan, who had been flying in from Tennessee. It was Allie's idea that they dress up like hill-billies in overalls, with blacked-out teeth. They were quite a sight. Cooper took comfort in the knowledge that her aunt would be a little less obvious.

Out in front of the terminal she thought she saw Penny's car several times, but each one was driven by someone Cooper didn't know. After several false alarms she pulled her suitcase over to a bench and sat down to wait, figuring that Penny must be caught in traffic or something. Then, just as she got comfortable she heard someone calling her name. But when she looked up it wasn't Penny or even Brian. It was Ryan Stewart, Cooper noticed as her heart dropped down into her shoes.

And he was holding a bouquet of flowers.

She approached him cautiously, trying to clear the confusion from her mind.

"Are you here picking someone up?" she asked, realizing how dumb the words sounded as soon as they were out of her mouth. "I mean, obviously you're here picking someone up, but, umm...." She continued to stammer for several seconds before finally blurting out "What are you doing here?"

"I came for you," was all he said.

21

ait a minute," Cooper said trying to remain calm. She didn't take the flowers Ryan offered so he was still holding them out in front of him. She couldn't help thinking that he looked strange, standing there on the sidewalk, holding a bouquet. "What do you mean you're here for me?"

"Your aunt is stuck in California. She's okay, but her timing belt went out this afternoon. It's being replaced but I guess it will be a while. She called your room an hour ago hoping she might catch Emily there. Lucky for you, I had just dropped her off. Emily asked if she could borrow the truck, but I volunteered for the job instead."

"I sure am lucky," Cooper agreed, feeling anything but. Maybe having Allie and the gang embarrassing her wouldn't have been so bad. Ryan made a move to help Cooper hoist her bags into the bed of the truck, but she ignored him and did it herself. He backed away after that, holding his hands up in surrender before unlocking her door and hopping behind the wheel.

"So how was your vacation?" Ryan asked once they were on the freeway. Cooper was amazed. After everything that had happened how could he just expect to have a casual conversation? She had thought she would at least get a chance to catch her breath before having to see Ryan again. He finally seemed to notice her silence.

"Cooper, are you planning on ignoring me all the way back to school?"

Cooper still didn't answer. She was trying to decide what, if anything, she wanted to say. It didn't help that the flowers were staring up at her from where they lay discarded on the truck's worn bench seat.

"How come you never brought me flowers when we were dating?" Cooper couldn't believe the words actually escaped her lips. She had really wanted to say something mature, something adult; instead, she was whining about his not bringing her flowers before.

"I know," Ryan replied eagerly, as if he were afraid she might stop talking again if he didn't answer fast enough. "I should have brought you flowers before. I should have done a lot of things before, but I'm trying to change."

"Do we really have to talk about this right now?" Cooper told him, trying to avoid the confrontation she knew was coming. The wounds from their break-up were just starting to heal for her, and now it felt like Ryan was picking at the scab.

"No, but I'd like to," Ryan answered. "You got my postcard, didn't you?"

"Yes," Cooper answered wearily. They were trapped together in the truck for the next thirty minutes. It appeared that she would be forced to talk about "them" if she didn't want to jump out at the next stoplight.

"I meant what I said. I think I was wrong," Ryan admitted.

Cooper hadn't realized how different it would sound to hear him actually say those words out loud. For a minute, she closed her eyes and let herself pretend that everything was okay...that the last three weeks hadn't happened. But eventually she had to open her eyes.

"You know, if you had said that to me the week after we broke up, I would have been thrilled," Cooper said.

"And now?"

"Last week when I got your postcard I was so mad that I wanted to hurt you the same way you hurt me, but now I'm starting to think maybe you were right to break up with me in the first place."

"But I *wasn't* right," Ryan argued.

"How do you know? What made you change your mind?"

"Because I missed you too much for it to have been right."

"I miss you, too," Cooper reluctantly admitted, "but maybe that's not enough. You know, I did things this last week that I all but gave up doing while you and I were together, and I realized how much I missed them."

"You can still do them when we're together!" Ryan insisted.

"Maybe, but I don't because they're not important to you. And I have to admit that a lot of the things you care about aren't important to me, no matter how hard I try to make them be."

"But you said if we worked on things a little you thought we could find a compromise," Ryan reminded her.

"I think we've found it: we stay good friends," Cooper told him, with more resolve than she was actually feeling.

She hoped Ryan would let it go at that, because she didn't know how much longer she could keep saying no to him. It had been fairly easy to put him out of her mind when she was thousands of miles away, but with him sitting right next to her it was decidedly harder.

They rode the rest of the way to PCU in silence, with Cooper forcing herself not to wipe at the few tears that had managed to escape. She didn't want Ryan to see she was crying.

Finally, after what seemed like hours, they pulled up in front of Cooper's dorm.

"Can I still call you sometimes?" Ryan asked, setting her suitcase on the sidewalk for her. Cooper didn't trust herself to speak so she just nodded her head.

Before she could escape, Ryan pulled her close to him and as he squeezed her tight one last time she breathed in that clean scent she had always loved, a combination of his soap, shaving cream, and laundry detergent. That simple smell was almost enough to make her take back everything she had just said, so she quickly untangled herself, whispered a barely audible "good-bye," and practically ran to her room.

"I am *so* sorry about letting Ryan pick you up," Emily said as soon as Cooper was through the door. "I tried to come myself, but he wouldn't give me the keys."

"It's okay," Cooper told her, throwing her stuff down on her unmade bed. Her room was just as she left it after exams: clothes thrown all over the floor, books scattered across her desk, a half-eaten rice cake on her bookshelf.

"But you look really upset," Emily pointed out gently.

"I am, but I'll be fine."

"I told him to leave you alone! I'm going to call that brother of mine and have a little talk with him."

Emily strode purposefully to the phone, but Cooper blocked her path.

"Don't. It's really not his fault. It's not anyone's fault, that's the problem. If I had someone to blame for how horrible I feel I don't think I'd feel so horrible."

"That makes sense, I think," Emily said, seeming to puzzle through her roommate's words.

"So how was your spring break?" Cooper asked, managing

to effectively change the subject.

"Let's me just sum it up by saying you are so lucky that you're an only child!" Emily said. "My sister drove me completely crazy the whole week."

The girls sat on Emily's neatly made bed and talked about their week apart, carefully avoiding the "R" word until bedtime.

Morning and the return to classes came much too soon. Cooper found it harder than she remembered to sit through an hour-long lecture, then at lunchtime she saw Ryan. It was just from a distance—he was standing across the cafeteria talking to one of his basketball teammates—but she still felt that little twinge of disappointment and her stomach dropped. She wondered if that would ever go away.

Walking into photography class, Cooper ran into Sam. Not having seen him since the hospital, she felt a little awkward. He didn't seem to, though.

"Hey, Cooper! Glad to be back?" he asked.

"I'm not sure," Cooper answered honestly.

"Yeah, I know what you mean," he replied, although Cooper doubted that he could actually understand her mixed feelings. "I want you to know Rachel didn't stop talking about you the rest of the night. I think you've got a friend for life."

"So does she."

"She'll be glad to hear that! And by the way, I want to thank you again for going out of your way. It was really great of you," he said, his eyes locking with hers.

"Like I said before, it was no big deal."

"It was a big deal to my sister, though, and she made me promise that I'd take you out to dinner to pay you back."

"Oh, you really don't have to do that," Cooper told him.

"I know I don't, but I want to."

"Really, it's not necessary," Cooper continued to protest. "You don't owe me anything."

"It wouldn't have to be like a date or anything if that's what you're worried about," Sam explained. "Your boyfriend has nothing to worry about."

"I don't have a boyfriend anymore so that isn't a problem," Cooper told him then watched his eyes grow wide with surprise.

"You and Ryan broke up? Really?" Sam asked a bit too happily.

"Before break," she explained. "Before exam week actually."

"Then I take it back, it would be a date," Sam said and it was Cooper's turn to be surprised.

"Um...I'm not really ready to date yet."

"Oh, come on," Sam urged. "You mean you're going to put your own feelings before the wishes of a sick little girl?" he joked.

"That is really low," Cooper said, with just a hint of a smile. "I can't believe you would use your sister's condition to take advantage of me in a weak moment just to get a date."

"Well believe it," he said without remorse. "Is it working?"

"No, it's not." She forced herself to look stern.

"I suppose I'll just have to call her at the hospital and tell her you said no to her one simple request," he continued.

"Don't you dare. I'll go. But you tell Rachel I'm doing this for her, not for you, so don't expect me to be any fun."

"I completely respect that," Sam said with a grin. "Tomorrow night at seven?"

"McNeil Hall. I'll meet you out front." she offered, already wondering what she had gotten herself into.

"And you might want to wear a dress," he added.

For some inexplicable reason Cooper found herself smiling as she walked back to her dorm after class.

22

ou have a date?" Emily asked. "With who?"

"It's not really a date," Cooper protested, but in her heart she knew it was, and she had to admit she was sort of looking forward to it. That admission made her feel like a horrible person, though, because how could she want to go out with someone else so soon after her break-up with Ryan? She pushed her feelings of guilt to the back of her mind.

"Where did you get that dress?" Emily asked in amazement.

"My friend Claire made it for me last week, it was a project for one of her classes," Cooper explained, smoothing down the fabric.

"Well it's gorgeous," Emily said then added, "especially for a *non-date*."

"I already feel weird enough, don't make it worse," Cooper pleaded with her roommate. "Sam wanted to thank me for spending the day with his little sister who happens to be in the hospital. It's not a big deal."

"Whatever you say."

Out at the curb a few minutes later Cooper kept telling herself the same thing. "It's not a big deal. It's not a big deal. It's not a big deal." She was still chanting those words when Sam pulled up to the curb.

"Is this yours?" Cooper asked as she climbed into the blue vintage Mustang Sam was driving. She was trying to recall if she had ever seen it parked in front of The Perfect Bagel, but she didn't think so.

"I borrowed it from a friend," he explained. "I didn't think you'd appreciate riding on the back of my scooter."

"Good call," Cooper told him.

"Look," Sam began before they were even out of the parking lot, "I know I sort of forced you into having dinner with me and while I would be really disappointed, I'd understand if you didn't really want to go."

"Well, good night then," Cooper said as she reached for the door handle.

Sam slammed on the breaks and turned to look at her. His shocked expression turned to a smile, though, when Cooper started laughing.

"I was just kidding. We're both here. We might as well go have dinner. Besides, I'm really hungry." What she didn't tell him was that her stomach was one huge knot of nerves.

"Great. I hope you like Italian food because I found this place called Bizarro—don't be put off by the name—up in the Fremont district, and I've been dying to try it. I'll warn you, it's sort of a converted garage, but it's really cool inside," he explained smiling at her.

Cooper had to keep telling herself not to look at his eyes because every time she did, her stomach began doing cart-wheels.

"I'll try to keep an open mind," she told him, while looking out the passenger window, pretending to be suddenly very interested in the traffic.

The restaurant didn't really having a parking lot, so they ended up parking at the bank across the street. Once inside, however, it was even better than Sam had promised. There was an entire picnic hanging from the ceiling with a red checkered tablecloth and everything. Ivy, flowers, and other miscellanea were wound around that.

Sam took her by the arm as they were led to a table by the wall, and Cooper was reminded of when he had held her arm at the hospital. She felt the same tingling sensation again.

Even after they were seated Cooper couldn't stop looking around. Having something to look at besides Sam helped put her more at ease. There was a mural on one wall and a stained-glass window hung like a picture on another. From her seat, she got a different view of the ceiling, and she noticed a fifteen-foot-long violin hanging over her head.

"So what do you think?" Sam asked.

"It's great in a very claustrophobic Michelangelo-gone-wild kind of way. It's perfect."

"I knew it!" Sam said triumphantly. "Some girls might think it was a little too weird, but I just knew you'd get it."

"I don't know if I get it, but I love it," Cooper admitted, enjoying his praise all the same.

Then without discussing it first they both ordered the special, a smoked mozzarella ravioli in a tomato-basil sauce. Looking from table to table there wasn't anything Cooper saw that didn't look appetizing, but still the ravioli sounded the best.

Looking around again, Cooper couldn't help thinking that this was exactly what she had wanted from Ryan on their anniversary, which only made her feel more guilty. They weren't together anymore and technically he had done the breaking up, but still she felt strange being out with another guy. And no matter what she tried to tell herself, she knew now it was very much a date.

"So how's your sister doing?" Cooper asked, trying to steer the conversation away from date-related topics.

"I talked to her today and she sounded fine. She said to tell you 'hi', too, and that she hopes you have a nice dinner."

So much for that idea, Cooper thought.

"I'm going to write and tell her all about it so you better be on your best behavior," Cooper warned Sam.

"I'm always on my best behavior, but that would be great if you wrote her. She starts chemotherapy again this week and any diversions are appreciated."

"Wow," Cooper said. "It sure puts my problems in perspective, doesn't it?"

"What problems?" Sam asked, leaning in as if Cooper were about to tell him a secret.

"Nothing, really. It's just that I have this appointment tomorrow that I'm really worried about," she confided. She didn't know why she was telling him any of this, but she couldn't seem to stop herself.

"What kind of appointment? Are you sick?" he asked in a worried tone.

"No, nothing like that. You see, I told you it was silly."

"So tell me anyway. We have some time to kill until the ravioli gets here."

"Okay, but remember you asked. There's this modeling agency here in Seattle—it's called Bella and it's right near campus—and I have an appointment with them tomorrow during my lunch break to discuss them taking me on while I'm not in New York."

"And you're afraid they might say no?" he questioned.

"Yes," Cooper admitted, "but it's not like it sounds. You see, a few months ago I would have been glad if they said no, but now I want to model for different reasons and I'm afraid that I'm going to get a door slammed in my face."

"What are these other reasons?" Sam asked. "Can you tell me?"

Cooper went on to explain the whole thing to Sam: from running into Jacinta and going to Models for Christ to her afternoon with Rachel at Sloan-Kettering. They were halfway through with their dinner by the time she finished.

"So do you get it now? Before it didn't matter if I worked or not, but now I feel like maybe I can make some kind of difference in the industry, even if it's only a small difference."

"And you're afraid that now that you've finally found this opportunity, it's going to be taken away from you," Sam finished for her.

"Exactly!"

"Cooper, I think you have to trust that God knows what He's doing."

"I know that God knows what He's doing; it's me I'm worried about."

"Well, stop. Look at all that's taken place in the last few weeks and all God had to do to change your mind about modeling. If something happens tomorrow and this agency says they won't take you, you have to know there will be a good reason."

As Cooper was nodding her agreement he added, "but I don't think that's going to happen."

Cooper was so glad he didn't just dismiss her concerns as nerves or offer some false compliment, like "they'd be crazy not to take someone as pretty as you." This was about more than that, and she was relieved that someone understood.

"Thanks. I didn't mean to monopolize the conversation all

night, but I have to say, I did warn you."

"You didn't monopolize the conversation at all. I'm honored that you felt you could confide in me."

"You're easy to talk to for some reason," Cooper told him as he paid the bill and escorted her out to his borrowed car.

Cooper felt less nervous on the ride home and was glad Sam didn't try to make conversation. Instead, as they drove down Aurora Avenue she looked out at Lake Union and allowed herself to be mesmerized by the lights dancing on the water. They were back on campus all too soon.

"Look, I know you have a lot going on right now," Sam said after walking Cooper to her door, "but is there any chance I might get you to go out with me again, of your own free will this time?"

Cooper tried to sort out her conflicting emotions. Not too long ago she didn't even like Sam, and now she thought he was great. But she was nowhere near being over Ryan yet, and in two more months it would be summer…and what would happen then?

"I really don't know," she finally replied.

"I understand, and I know this is really fast, but I think you also know I've liked you for a while now. I don't mind waiting around for a little while longer if that's what you want. But, Cooper, if you don't think of me like that, I hope you'll be honest enough to tell me."

"Honestly? I don't know what I think. I mean I had a really nice time and I think I do like you, but at the same time I feel guilty for liking you."

"Well that's honest," Sam said.

"I just don't think I'm ready to dive into another relationship."

"Then let's start with what you are ready for. What would

you be comfortable with?" Sam asked, unwilling to give up so easily.

Cooper thought it over for a minute then blurted out, "Bagels!"

"You'd be comfortable with bagels?" Sam asked. "I don't get it."

"We can get together for bagels," Cooper proposed. "That's not too much pressure on me, and it's not a formal date. Also, they're cheap," she told him with a smile.

"Bagels, huh?" Sam repeated.

"Bagels and the Sunday *New York Times*," Cooper said. "And I get to read the Arts & Entertainment section first. That's the offer: take it or leave it."

"Okay, bagels it is," Sam replied eagerly, not even pretending to think it over. "When?"

"Whenever," Cooper said. "We don't have to nail this down right now, do we?"

"No, but I think I had better warn you: I see a lot of bagels in your future."

"We'll see," Cooper said. "We'll see."

N U M B E R **1**
FRESHMAN BLUES

By Wendy Lee Nentwig
ISBN 0-88070-947-2

Emily Stewart has looked forward to her freshman year at PCU for years. But things don't go quite as planned. When Emily's best friend loses her financial aid, Emily finds herself rooming instead with a sloppy New Yorker named Cooper. Not only that, but Em has to deal with her over-protective brother (who decides to date Cooper!), peer pressure, new friends, and college deadlines...not to mention inedible dorm food.

Further complications arise when Emily meets what may be the man of her dreams. At first, John Wehmeyer seems to be exactly the type of guy she has been waiting for: gorgeous, romantic, and a Christian! Best of all, John thinks that Emily is wonderful, too. But when conflicts arise, Emily learns the hard way that true love is about more than romance.

Yet, even as a frightening and climactic confrontation leaves her stranded far from campus, Emily makes exciting discoveries about herself and rediscovers an incredible source of strength that will see her through her *Freshman Blues* and beyond.

N U M B E R **2**
HOMEWARD HEART

By Lissa Halls Johnson
ISBN 0-88070-948-0

Maddy MacDonald's first year at PCU brings yet another new beginning for the girl who spent her childhood moving from town to town. This time, however, quirky Maddy has made up her mind to set down roots. Unfortunately, that's easier said than done after she finds herself in all kinds of trouble—trouble that threatens her future at PCU.

As it turns out, Maddy's fun-loving boyfriend, Kick, may love fun just a little too much—and he seems determined to get Maddy to join him in his adventures. Yet, even as Maddy strives to avoid the party scene, her mere association with Kick may provide exactly the ammunition a disgruntled coworker needs to get her booted out of the library—and the school—for good.

Will an unfortunate misunderstanding lead to her dismissal from the college? Or will Maddy finally find an anchor for her *Homeward Heart*?

Available at your local Christian bookstore.
If it is not in stock, ask them to special order it for you!

NUMBER 3
TRUE IDENTITY

By Bernie Sheahan
ISBN 0-88070-949-9

Kenzie Dawson, the Nashville-born-and-bred daughter of a Christian record company president, is using PCU as an escape from the pressures that come with being in the Christian music industry's inner circle. How long can she keep up the charade?

Kenzie finds that her reluctance to share the details of her Nashville life with her new PCU friends soon gets in the way. But it takes a budding romance with the musically talented Chris Gallagher, a Seattle concert appearance of longtime family friend and Christian pop star Billy Weber, and an ongoing tense relationship with Emily Stewart—her "Christian music freak" suitemate—to force Kenzie to make some difficult choices regarding the kind of person she wants to be.

Will she finally embrace her background, her Nashville life, and her own remarkable musical gifts? Or will she continue to hide the truth from her new friends, in hopes of creating a new image for herself, apart from her Nashville associations? Meet the real Kenzie Dawson in *True Identity*.

Available after September 1996 at your local Christian bookstore.
If it is not in stock, ask them to special order it for you!